The Very Thought of Education

THE VERY THOUGHT OF EDUCATION

PSYCHOANALYSIS AND THE IMPOSSIBLE PROFESSIONS

DEBORAH P. BRITZMAN

STATE UNIVERSITY OF NEW YORK PRESS

Published by
STATE UNIVERSITY OF NEW YORK PRESS
ALBANY

© 2009 State University of New York

For information, contact
State University of New York Press, Albany NY
www.sunypress.edu

Production, Laurie Searl
Marketing, Fran Keneston

Library of Congress Cataloging-in-Publication Data

Britzman, Deborah P., 1952–
    The very thought of education : psychoanalysis and the impossible
professions / Deborah P. Britzman.
       p. cm.
    Includes bibliographical references and index.
    ISBN 978-1-4384-2645-7 (hardcover : alk. paper)
    ISBN 978-1-4384-2646-4 (paperback : alk. paper)
    1. Learning, Psychology of.   2. Psychoanalysis and education.
    I. Title.
    BF318.B787 2009
    370.15—dc22   2008042785

10 9 8 7 6 5 4 3 2 1

CONTENTS

PREFACE

Everything "started" when I had nothing more to say, when I no longer knew where to end or how to end. At that moment, what I had recounted before came back, but in a way that was entirely other, in a discontinuous way, in different forms (memories, dreams, slips, repetitions), or it never came back. I understood that I had tried, by telling the story of "my life," not to recount it—it is too much for words—but to master it. I had been at once foolish and unfaithful.

—Sarah Kofman, "'My Life' and Psychoanalysis"

Freud's (1900) book of dreams handed psychoanalysts more than a few clues as to the utter difficulty of undergoing its strange education. He suggested that even in our sleep there is work to be done and in waking life dream work may well be the transfer point for our bungled actions, slips, jokes, misreading, wild thoughts, and memories. Through insisting that the dream is both other to conscious life and a commentary on it, by lifting the curtain of his own dream theater to present what is unfaithful, foolish, and inadmissible in rational life, by reading between these lines and even finding that which is not there at all, by remembering the forgotten as signifying remnants of missed meaning, and so, by starting with what is most unintentional, Freud asked those learning psychoanalysis to become students of their ignorance. We are asked to take the side of the wish for this other world by associating with it and greeting this curiosity with warm regard. Kofman's (2007b) fragment of her analysis struggles with another sense of what psychoanalysis feels like: without reason, bereft words return the speaker's agony.

One hundred years later, many analysts think of Freud's (1900) chapter six, "The Dream Work," as the text's navel, the bodily excess that stands for what can never happen again. Having to be born will signify our unrepresentable beginning, and our relation to the other. It will be felt as what Kofman describes as "too much for words." Yet if the psychoanalyst may only ask for what is uncertain in words—putting unthinkable things into them and calling into speech that which is not speech—the request creates more than words can say. The paradox of dreams, and thus of psychoanalysis, is that words return a foreign self; however eloquent, wild, or harsh these words feel, they turn the speaker over to what is most enigmatic, most unresolved, and perhaps irresolvable in her or his life.

From the perspective of what cannot be consciously noticed but continues to impress, the dream work compresses, distorts, displaces, reverses, fragments, and envisages the day's residues with our unfilled wishes. It plays havoc with beginning language, as if each night we learn words for the first time. Dreams are utterly literal, in the sense that they say what they mean without meaning what they say. They arrange what Freud (1900) noticed as "a thing that is *capable of being represented*" (340) and, in this way, propose our best suggestions. Yet dreams are ambiguous and with this claim Freud will tell us that the method of their interpretation will suffer from the radical indeterminacy of its subject and object, that the wishes dreams somehow create cannot be met with the analyst's suggestion of how to think of them. Any interpretation will be speculative and uncertain (Kohon 1986b). In the case of dreams and in the case of education, considerations of representability will only mean that something unknown is being presented. And dreams, Freud writes, *"are not made with the intention of being understood"* (341). This radical condition impresses the form, style, and force of both the method of dreams and their interpretation. In this transference, both analyst and analysand are affected.

Freud was telling us that, just as with the dream work, the psychoanalyst, along with the analysand, would be caught between not knowing and the desire to know, and by creating a transfer of love into knowledge this conflict begins their strange education. The nature of this education, however, is not easy to convey because it exists and does not exist at the same time. This unusual tendency places psychoanalysis in the defenseless position of inviting uncertainty and gambling with nonsense without losing its patience. At the very least, and like the dream, psychoanalysis provides a frame to consider our uncertainty by working through the order of anxiety that destroys our capacity to think. The central theme of *The Very Thought of Education* begins with the idea that, like the dream, education requires association, interpretation, and a narrative capable of bringing to awareness, for further construction, things that are farthest from the mind. And whatever education is dedicated to, all education suffers a radical fate of indeterminacy. The approach that can best turn education inside out, in order to understand something of its emotional situation and its inhibitions, symptoms, and anxieties, is psychoanalysis.

In any learning one feels pressure, without knowing from where it comes, to make knowledge certain and so to stabilize the object lest it escape one's efforts. This fight with knowledge meets its limits in anguish over the loss of certainty, a loss needed in order to symbolize what is new. In the dream work of education, we act without knowing in advance what becomes of our efforts and meet again ignorance and hubris, but also our passion and desire. We hope that education can help us out of this mess and worry that education is this mess. We can, with confidence, admit that because learning is always an emotional situation, the very thought of education animates our phantasies of knowledge, authority, and love. Uncertainty—itself the core of life—plays with the meaning of education. Where psychoanalysis departs from other styles of understanding may be in its willingness to create within its practices a love affair with what is at most difficult to love: our uncertain beginnings and times when understanding must fail. Without condition, psychoanalysis may welcome these difficulties.

My understanding of education's becoming—and what becomes of education as one undergoes it—has been affected by going back to school: this time, to learn to become a psychoanalyst. Psychoanalytic training involves me with didactic seminars, with seeing patients, with being supervised, and with my own analysis. Each dimension of this education seems to demand my love and hate, that is, the transference with the difficulties, discontinuities, and conflicts that this education must present. Readers will find these affected glimmers in the chapters that follow. But there are sidelines.

In the middle of writing this book I had a dream that seemed to bring into relief what psychoanalytic education can feel like:

> I was in a classroom, seated at a table, facing a female psychologist who was examining me. I may have been in the fourth year class of the Psychoanalytic Institute where I am a candidate. My classmates looked on indifferently. The psychologist asks me what instrument I use to clinically assess my patients. I can't think of anything except the Rorschach test, but feel that must be the wrong answer. I go dumb and cannot say anything to the examiner.

I suppose some of this dream comments on my feelings of insecurity and wishes to measure up. I do not have a background in either the field of medicine or psychology and there has always been, in the history of psychoanalytic training, a question of what qualifies the lay analyst to do this work. The other tension is whether psychoanalysis is on the side of art or science (Kohon

1986a). Yet, as a beginner, this dream may also signify my worries of how my patients assess me. Or maybe the dream frames my feelings about my psycho-analytic education when I feel caught between a desire for mastery and a wish not to know and where the transfer point is my ignorance. Perhaps the wish is to be corrected or to be given a magical instrument that will settle it all. The Rorschach test is not one of errors and corrections, but an invitation to free association. It is composed of abstract images with the invitation to read between its lines and narrate what cannot be there: our remainders. In free association, there is no such thing as a wrong answer; yet in the dream I can-not associate for fear of being wrong. The examiner is asking me something I know nothing about, taunting me with her certainty and my ignorance. In a fight with my own psychology, words fail.

In the analyst's consulting room, speech takes hold of what is extraor-dinary to its function: one word leads to another by way of what was never intended. Meaning seems to lose its grip; one gets lost in words, or loses words, or messes them up. If there is no such thing as an accident, it is only because what is most accidental about us creates the psychoanalytic land-scape. Things communicated are well beyond what one thinks one is saying because of the enigmatic unconscious, because of the properties of language itself, because of the transference, and because of the other who listens with a free-floating attention and ideally, with an understanding of the fragility of making emotional contact. The other touches my words, without knowing in advance what becomes of meaning. An early goal of psychoanalysis was to make the unconscious conscious. Then, it became a working through of resis-tance to psychoanalysis. More modestly, there was the goal of moving from neurosis to ordinary misery. Still later, some supposed the goal was to make psychoanalytic contact and open both the analyst and the analysand to their respective differences as they meet the unknown. Others will pose the work as learning to play and to dream. Learning the truth of one's desire would be another elusive goal, as would the capacity to find something novel and new or even to write one's own story. It is noteworthy to remark that there is no agreement as to its goal. But there is also no goal that can settle what mean-ings a self who dreams can create.

The analytic setting invites our transference, the troubles in learning, and contains them in the playground of words. But the force of old con-flicts startles the work. They are painful to remember, turn on negation, and express what is felt before it can be known. There are worries of falling, fears of being misunderstood, and phantasies that the analyst will throw one out. One is bored and worries the other knows this. One falls asleep. The most disorganized parts of a self are presented and disclaimed, berated and forgiven. Considerations of representation come to feel as inconsiderate representations. How strange these worries feel to conscious life, for no evidence can secure their cause, there is nothing that causes the cause, the evidence at stake seems mere, or what feels like a reason collapses into an excuse. What, after all, is the proof of feelings? Without justification, I report my dreams and feel my own strangeness. Their literalness is astounding and, on better days, they make me laugh. I dream I am being introduced before my important lecture as "Professor of Sausage." I dream I am losing my grip and cannot do chin-ups. I cannot pull myself up. "Losing your grip," the analyst replies, "this is our work." I think, "Oh great. I am swimming in a sea of vulnerability and words are barely strong enough to lend me a life raft. I am sinking between words." My psychoanalyst invites me to let go with free association. It is all so difficult. I am embarrassed that while a great deal of my work and writing concerns the pedagogy of uncertainty, I cannot stand my own feelings of not knowing what to do. I want my analyst to tell me what to do, to help me. I have confused needing help with wanting her to take away my bad feelings. We both know telling me what to do will only lead to more resistance. All at once I feel old and young.

All of this confusion between good and bad, between help and authority, between the past and the present, and between words and things, I believe, belongs to the educator's dilemma, with the exception that the educational setting, more often than not, becomes flummoxed by how free association unravels its memories of certainty. And yet, as with analysis, much of what goes on in education is the transference, the uncertain exchange of confusion, love, and words. Many of us who teach, whether in compulsory school settings, in the university, or in psychoanalytic institutes, consciously accept the fact that the work of education is as difficult for us as it is for our students, that a great deal of what occurs in seminars and classrooms seems beyond conscious reach, that in the midst of unfolding pedagogy, more often than not, we become undone. Many accept the fact that we do not know what is going on or even how we feel about it, that students puzzle us or make us mad, and that however much we plan in advance, however clear our lesson plans feel to us, whatever beauty our syllabus design mirrors, however narcissistic we may feel in conveying knowledge or however much we attempt to convey our understanding to others or strain to receive the other's inchoate views, the pedagogical encounter and what becomes of it are radically unstable, subject to the unconscious and the dream work. From the other side, students are involved in their own transference with the teacher, the material, some archaic, demanding other and, to the education they did not have. They may wish the teacher to leave them alone, or come closer, or tell them what she wants. They may not want to know anything about it, or demand to be given the proper instrument that will come with some sort of guarantee. They may be anxious about measuring up or feel too big and too smart. There is so much going on that we do not know about or do not want to know anything about. Experience cannot protect us from our conflicts and uncertainties since experience itself is conflictive and uncertain and requires our speculative interpretations.

In some sense, what education feels like is as difficult to convey as what psychoanalysis feels like. They have that in common. Their respective emotional situations as well share in the fact that, because they are so needed, both are deeply misunderstood and perhaps feared. If both fields of practice require our representation, there remains something unrepresentable about learning them. This aporia is what we learn over and over through trying to represent what is missing but nonetheless refines our desire. While there are particular skills and techniques that may help us out of a mess, they cannot help us with how the mess feels or even judge whether the mess is needed. And besides, the unrepeatable encounters made in both fields mean that our experience is always new experience fighting with the old. On this view, it is difficult indeed to say how we are affected by learning to live and how it happens that when it comes to the very thought of education, we often feel the need to be certain without ever wondering why.

While working on this book, I was fortunate to receive a number of important invitations to present aspects of this work, learn how well psychoanalysis travels, and think more about the problems education gives. While the errors in this book belong to me, I'd like to acknowledge the 2006 Canadian Association of Teacher Education meeting and Professor M. Meyer of the University of Hamburg, Germany, for their respective invitations to share my work in the psychoanalysis of learning. Thanks to the American Education Studies Association for inviting me to give the 2006 Kneller Lecture and to the invitation to present in 2007 to the International Federation for Psychoanalytic Education, held in Toronto. Special thanks to Dr. A. Sahin of the MEF School in Istanbul, Turkey, who invited me to participate in the first conference in psychoanalysis and education held at the school. The topic of the 2007 conference was rethinking education, and its clinical orientation continues to inspire my work. My gratitude goes to those who taught me the clinical intricacies of psychoanalytic listening: specifically I thank Dr. M. Flax and Dr. J. Levy. I am lucky to have colleagues who care deeply for the psychoanalytic life and the conflicts invited. I thank Professor C. Zemel who heard most of this book and gave good advice. I have benefited from conversations with Dr. O. Gozlan, and Professors Sliwinski and Lather. Thanks also must go to Jane Banker, editor in chief at the State University of New York Press. My gratitude again goes to Professor Pitt whose generosity, love, and keen sense of life in education makes my life better. A short version of chapter two originally appeared in the *International Journal of Leadership in Education* and part of chapter three appeared in *Changing English*. I thank Taylor and Francis Publishers for their permission to draw upon this earlier work.

CHAPTER ONE

THE VERY THOUGHT

It is almost impossible to imagine the work of thinking, speaking, listening, reading, and writing without stumbling into the history of one's education. The very thought directs a timeless affected world. We may be reminded of how uncertain its certainties felt and then turn to the incalculability of its accidents, mistakes, and unmarked events. Then, too, this transference may multiply disreputable education since, more often than not, education and what becomes of learning tend to be symbolically equated with correction, completion, and with the bringing up of culture, knowledge, and life. Even as we fight against the ways progress is its watchword, goal, vulnerability, and contention, we may find ourselves falling behind. And when memories such as those we felt we had long ago discarded suddenly return what is incomplete in this education, we may find ourselves trying to shrug them off, for, after all, they carry clouds of regret, shame, and even sadness. To wonder how the very thought of this education impresses our desire for meaning, our phantasies of knowledge and the other, our questions of origin and existence, our sense of a profession and its learning, and, from all of this, our relation to the world, imagining this education may find its limit in the capture of compulsory schooling and memories of a child waiting there. It is as if the very thought of education will never let us go beyond what has already happened and so refuses to grow up.

Our childhood of education is one reason the very thought of education cannot seem to leave school and why education feels so concrete. No doubt, compulsory school life—having to grow up there, passing through its grades, and encountering an avalanche of certainty through its measures of success and failure—configures how we consider literal education. But however adhesive memory life in school turns out to be, the origin of the thought of education cannot be found there. Long before we enter the classroom we have already been written upon by what Hannah Arendt (1993a) simply called "the fact of natality"(61): that we are born and enlivened by our first other's readings, which leave in its wake our capacity for the transference, nascent interpretations telegraphing our needs, demands, and desires. This impressive education registers our drama of dependency, helplessness, and love, all lost and found in the transference: in hopes for what language, knowledge, and the other can bring. Affected education will take Arendt (1993b) to the problem of beginnings with her claim that "the essence of education is natality, the fact that human beings are *born* into the world" (174). And this will bring us into the paradox that while the needed experience of education somehow forms thought, the very thought of education is difficult to think. The psychoanalyst Wilfred Bion (1997) will make stranger education's natality when he proposed a constitutive alienation in the name of "wild thoughts," or "thoughts without a thinker (27)."[1] What could cause the thought of education to take place within us yet leave us feeling as if its events happened without our knowing why?

To bind education to its own unthought, to make a case for the idea that something within education resists thinking, that there is something about education that one knows nothing about, may seem counterintuitive to the project of education since ostensibly, education is a deliberation, a judgment, and, oddly, a result of itself. Yet as both experience and as institution, as training ground and as learning life, and as natality and its repression, people who are both undergoing education as they are directing others in their learning rarely think the thought of education. Instead, they may fall back into their knowledge and its transmission. This is one form of resistance, not to education or what happens to people as they influence one another, but to the incompleteness that education animates and disavows. And nowhere is this tension of incompleteness felt with more force than when we think the thought of education dynamically: as uneven development, as conflict, as promise, and as reparation. To bring into relief the contours of this education leads me to inquire into the particular education of adults: how it is that teachers, university professors, psychoanalysts, philosophers, artists, adult analysands, and even characters from novels confront unconscious life to learn from their inner world and feel that they need to know this world more deeply to overcome inhibitions, interpret reality, and create anew. Our guide to this world will be "the impossible professions," a formulation Freud (1925c) first rehearsed when he commented on the creative work of one of his colleagues in education.

Freud saw in the work of psychoanalysis, governance, and education the interminability of trying to influence others who have their own minds and tied these relations to practitioners' unconscious resistance, to the fact of their natality, and to their psychical life. Education itself will be interminable because it is always incomplete and because it animates our own incompleteness. And one can find "the education of education" within the stammers, conflicts, and dreams of adults who meet their otherness as they encounter the understanding of others. While education then will reference both procedures and unaccountable affects, the registration of education, more often than not, is dissociated from the very thought of education. And nowhere is this problem more poignant than when brought to consideration of the teacher's world that educates, as she or he is educated. We will see that there is a field called education that typically refers to the training of teachers. Then there is the experience of education that we associate with life's lessons, the accumulation of knowledge, and maybe the university. How these worlds separate and cut short the ways in which we imagine any education leads me to psychoanalysis, putting the very thought of education—including the one belonging to psychoanalysts—on the couch to invite free association and then read into its congealed matters. I ask readers to entertain the question of what it can mean to think the thought of education as experience, as pedagogy, as affect, as uneven development, as intersubjectivity, and as the basis of the transference and the countertransference. And we will relate these desires for love, recognition, and knowledge to that which resists it: thoughts that we are making too much of education.

The transference and countertransference are concepts worked with throughout this book. The psychoanalytic assumption is that there can be no learning without transference, but since the transference is also a needed obstacle to learning, it is subject to analysis, the work of deconstruction. These terms orient, construct, and obscure an understanding of how communication always conveys the otherness of conscious intent, and so touches a history without origin. The transference and countertransference reach into the problem of how language itself comes to gamble with its objects and our perceptions of them by way of wishes, phantasies, and anxieties and defenses. Imagine these words as characters in a psychoanalytic theater, as a play with the dispersal, force, and transformation of our affected unconscious history punctuated by our conscious attitude toward it. Their form will revive and revise conflicts of love and hate, transferred when we are with important others, when we fall in love, when we try to make the unfamiliar familiar, when we attempt to understand, and when we try to refind in the world images of our own likeness and difference. And the countertransference will be the educator's reply. The transference and the countertransference are also technical terms to understand psychoanalytic events from the perspective of the logic of affect with the question of what else libidinal ties, ambivalence, and scenes of hate made from being with others unconsciously convey. We can think of the transference and the countertransference as composing and decomposing a history of affected education, condensing and displacing time with what is unconscious.

When a sixty-year-old Freud (1914b) was asked how he came to choose his life work and so began by reflecting on his own schoolboy psychology, he presented a story of his transference to the authority of school and teachers, forever linking the transference to the very thought of education. This led him to notice his love affair with knowledge yet to be learned and his incredulity at having learned again that school still tugged on his mind. His opening remarks can be read as what the transference feels like:

> It gives you a queer feeling if, late in life, you are ordered once again to write a school essay. But you obey automatically like the old soldier who, at the word "Attention," cannot help dropping whatever he may have in his hands and who finds his little fingers pressed along the seams of his trousers. It is strange how readily you obey the orders, as though nothing particular had happened in the last half-century. But in fact you have grown old in the interval. (241)

In the next paragraph, Freud comments on the authority of these memories to turn the clock back and so "the present time seemed to sink into obscurity" (241) even as it still manages to affect what is remembered and repeated. Yet the repetition of feelings—in the form of needing to obey—is not the same as the old events now long gone: something more is yet to be understood when one tries to account for one's desire and its remainders, when one tries to think the immaterial material that shapes styles of love and hate, and thus of learning. If our capacity for the transference and the countertransference leaves us with the timeless presence of education, it is also the means for symbolizing how it is that education's return turns us into a child.

So difficult is it to imagine this florid scenery of education, so difficult is it to interpret this transference, that we would rather forget its erotic force. We do not typically begin with how identification with instituted education threads through our object world to affect what we come to call ethics, responsibility, care, and critique, and to how we feel these experiences internally. We may not often think that what resides within the heart of knowledge we either hold dear or attempt to expel into others is a dormant theory of its truth and, too, unconscious instructions as to how it can be or should be learned or avoided. We may not often associate the thought of education with an unconscious history of our infantile relations to theory, knowledge, and to others and as animated again in any educational relation. We may not often notice what else is communicated by the thought that we do not wish to know anything about it. And yet, for there to be any learning at all, our composition of learning begins with what is not a composition but a potential: existence.

Such an expansive sense of education is usually foreclosed by the very thought of education. More often than not, the very thought of education collapses our capacity to think with the thing-in-itself. How does the thought of this education become so small that it is mainly considered as a matter for instructing the inexperienced and as affecting only the young? Why does the thought of education stall in measures of success and failure? How then did this idea transfer to characterize the ways adults learn a profession or attempt self-understanding? Is there something about being educated, about undergoing education, that incurs our regression to infantile dependency and invites defenses against helplessness? If the experience of education overrides thinking the very thought of education, what problems are then inherited by learning the impossible professions? More simply, when it comes to the very thought of education, what is it like to feel one's beginnings over and over and to receive oneself and be received by others as if one has never had to start life?

We have noticed the difficulty Sigmund Freud had with his school assignment, his love and hate with authority, and his race with what remains timeless about his own time. It seems as though education is the transference and we may spend our lives trying to destroy its authority. Fifty years later, his daughter Anna Freud spoke of her education from the vantage of her teachers' countertransference, how she imagined her teachers saw her. Late in life, Anna Freud (1969) received an honorary degree of Doctor of Science from the Jefferson Medical College Medical School. At the time, she was sixty-nine years old. She was surprised at this unexpected turn of events and continually wondered, "Why me?" In her address upon receiving the honor, Anna Freud returned to her own psychoanalytic education that occurred before there were any established psychoanalytic institutes. Her psychoanalytic education relied on personal analysis, the seeing of patients, participation in study groups, and in a new psychoanalytic society her father, Sigmund Freud, organized in Vienna. By the time she received this award, Anna Freud would have founded her own curriculum on ego psychology in the British Psychoanalytical Society in London, oversaw and helped translate the collected works of Sigmund Freud, served as senior training analyst, and would continue to be in great demand as a consultant in the applied fields of law, education, and psychology, what Freud saw as "the impossible professions."

Anna Freud was a teacher by background and a "lay analyst" by profession. She did not have medical training and so represented a side of psychoanalysis unhinged from its authority. Both situations—her background in education and her work in psychoanalysis—may have influenced her humane definition of clinical experience as consisting of "practical contact with human beings" (512), a measure without time, credential, or institution. The Vienna Society, however, could not escape putting back into place the authoritative education of its senior members:

> For many years the analytic beginner in the Society was looked down on as "inexperienced." I remember that even the discussion group which we initiated among ourselves for the exchange of opinions was officially called the "Children's Seminar," not because child cases were discussed there, but because the discussants themselves were considered to be in analytic infancy. (513)

We can imagine this space of education made small by the teacher's countertransference, where students are looked down upon and oddly are introjected into the teacher's old self only to be projected back into the world in the form of needy infants. Is it the case that, even without a formal school setting, those who come before us have a need to send beginners, and thus their education, back to kindergarten?

Somehow, the idea of lived education becomes "a wild thought," a frustration that goes on without a thinker. When thoughts of education are not permitted to leave the classroom, a place that cannot think itself into being without our being there, the concept of education loses its allegorical force, its likeness to the transference and the countertransference, and its nonsemblance with the problem of learning to live with others. When education is reduced to its most literal time, it collapses into phantasy and idealization to foreclose our capacity to think the thought of education. Lost as well is the question of why any education is an encounter with what is not yet, an experience with what is most incomplete in us. To think the force of education in this way permits one to leave behind our relentless repetition of "inexperience" and attend to the problem of what it is to learn from having experience at all. To think the thought of education as a working through of phantasies of education asks a great deal of us since the character of education itself can neither live without reinstituting its own childhood nor leave that which follows from it: the avalanche of complaints, disappointments, narcissistic injuries, and "queer feelings" that all too often collapse the meaning of education with the classroom and its measures of success and failure and experience and inexperience. Without questions, education sinks into melancholia.

We can, however, interpret this case and be curious why it is so, why the idea of education has been so scaled down that it can only refer to what has already happened to us and then what needs to happen to inexperienced others. By putting something one does not want into the past and projecting these anxieties into others, one maintains the false hope that what has already happened no longer has any force to hurt one today. Anna Freud (1995) considered denial as the ego's defense against its own vulnerable certainty and as a fight with the nature of truth. Indeed, throughout her discussion of ego defenses, she raises the question of whether education must first invite neurosis to even wonder what lessons it could actually teach. We will see how the ego's defenses, animated by the fact of having to be educated, churn when educating others. We will see how education begins with the anxiety of dependency, helplessness, and fears of separation. This can mean that our defenses against thinking the thought of education, itself a temporary solution, somehow anticipate our educational dangers: dependency and the anxieties of having to relive the profound helplessness of one's infancy. Here, the fact of natality is a current of emotional life, electrifying the transference and the countertransference to education.

Whereas Anna Freud noted the infantilizing qualities of her analytic education, we can find this repetition of anxiety and defense in the university as well. It usually comes in the form of teaching, for example, when books that might make a difference to how one lives are treated as a still life (*Natura Morta*). Slavitt's (2007) translation of the Oedipus cycle carries a little warning to his readers. In his preface to Sophocles's *Theban Plays*, he writes: "I am mindful of the fact that some of the readers of this book may be students to whom it has been assigned. I apologize to them and hope they can somehow overlook that unfortunate compulsion and find ways to respond to Sophocles' poetry innocently—as if they had come to these pages voluntarily and even eagerly" (x). That education might ruin the Oedipus story is not without irony since Oedipus refused to be educated by the prophecy that he then accidentally, or unconsciously, carried out. After all, Oedipus was told that he would be king, but only after he murdered his father and married his mother. It was not until he completed the unspeakable that his tragedy could begin and that he could then think about his own hand in life.

Slavitt, however, is suggesting another fate for Oedipus when sent to school. There is a worry that readers who greet Oedipus may turn away from the problem of knowledge. If the tragedy plays through conventional rules of the pedagogical exchange, if the teacher treats the book as a thought without students, the unconscious dilemma of Oedipus will be strangely cut short: Oedipus will be killed off before he can have his terrible education. Our translator may be anxious about this particular transference, not with Oedipus, but with the authority of the classroom. Poor Oedipus may be lost again, and we may repeat a part of his fate, what will come to be called "the passion for ignorance." Whether there is any innocence to be recovered in our encounter with Oedipus may be a question of a different order; Slavitt's apology, however, bears witness to our educational misfortunes and the difficulty of becoming a volunteer in the free association of one's own learning.

Perhaps the largest misfortune that will concern us has to do with what the philosopher Alain Badiou (2005) in his discussion of art and philosophy saw as "the collapse of the pedagogic theme" (7). We have already noted its collapse in trying to symbolize the childhood of education without having to repeat it. The pedagogic theme is one that can hardly accompany the thought of education because, more often than not, pedagogy is presented as the great controlling emissary opposed to its own struggle for symbolization. With the collapse of the pedagogic theme, Badiou was pointing to a loss of faith in the idea of transmission, whether this transmission takes shape through the science of didacticism, the feelings of catharsis, or the philosophical romance with openings, all of which refer to the decline of Western philosophy to think the limits of its own thematic. The pedagogic theme is a condensation made from the idea that education refers to both the teaching of youth and thus is concerned with the problem of the transmission, and to that which ties knowledge to truth, a more intimate transference registering the Eros of encounter and ordering our desire for knowledge. By its nature, the pedagogic theme places knowledge and truth at odds and so contains a constitutive conflict. If the presence of pedagogy is as much a procedure of knowledge as it is a relation to the other, and as such is always entangled in the problem of truth, the transference to education means that knowledge will have to pass through affect, the residue of our questions of love and hate. And when truth attempts to assert itself through disavowing the love that put it into place, Badiou argues, it is truth that experiences a powerlessness: there is no truth that can be the whole truth and nothing but the truth. Procedures of knowledge will also contain the excess of affect: we meet exceptions, limits, anxieties, and desire.

Badiou imagines education as the link between art and philosophy, since both modes of expression suffer a pedagogical theme. Yet he also sees in art a possibility for education:

> Art is pedagogical for the simple reason that it produces truths and because "education" (save in its oppressive or perverted expressions) has never meant anything but this: to arrange forms of knowledge in such a way that some truth may come to pierce a hole in them.
>
> What art educates us for is therefore nothing apart from its own existence. The only question is that of *encountering* this existence, that is, of thinking through a form of thought [*penser une pensée*]. (9)

What educates us is our existence, which is perhaps why Badiou places in scare quotes the concept of education. Another question is hinted at by both Anna Freud and the translator Slavitt. Can education be saved from its perverted and oppressive tendencies, or must the pedagogic theme collapse in order for us to think it?

To encounter existence is another way of speaking about thinking. Badiou's education appears not as a thought of itself but as thinking thought itself, as existence. And one quality of thinking is that it arranges thought in such a way that doubt bothers knowledge procedures, tears truth with another truth. Here is where the pedagogic theme may collapse into what Slavitt (2007) saw as "that unfortunate compulsion" (x) of education, itself a feature of thought. The paradox comes after the collapse: when we analyze our history of education, we experience uneven development, regression, and repetition and education cannot direct itself to this existence, to what it is like to need education and to think what happens to thought within its own unfolding. What collapses this theme is education's forgetting of its own natality.

PSYCHOANALYTIC THEMATICS

Our theme involves the concept of education with the intimate problem of trying to encounter affected and affecting existence as our transference to learning to live. For psychoanalysis, education is both a human condition and the means to symbolize our conditions. It is both a force of depression and its antidepressant. Yet education poses a dilemma for psychoanalysis because however different these fields of practice are, however much psychoanalysis is concerned with freeing the mind from our educational illness, psychoanalysis is not immune from its own education. Conceptions of education will also be the psychoanalyst's illness, even as its therapeutic mode attempts to propose an education without authority or suggestion. With the help of Badiou's view of art, we will try to grasp the concept of education wherever it can be lost and found, and, indeed, claim that the refinding of education is predicated on its loss and negation. There will be conflicts in judgment's polarities, a fight between objectivity and subjectivity and between affirmation and destruction, and an odd thought called negation that comments on not thinking (Freud 1925b). Thus, a deep dilemma for any education will concern how to symbolize its work of refinding its lost objects.

To think the thought of education, I draw upon philosophy, literature, and psychoanalysis. Literature serves as my third term, used to open questions of loss, desire, and freedom. Since literature cannot be in charge of itself but charges us to think, a theory of reading will be needed to contain the problem of resistance to these subjective adventures. From psychoanalytic speculations, beginning with Freud and moving on to the formulations of the mind created by the object relations' theories of Melanie Klein, Donald Winnicott, and Wilfred Bion, we will explore the unworldly world of love and hate in thinking. On occasion, one of the psychoanalysts who had a great deal of criticism toward the epistemology of psychoanalytic education, Jacques Lacan, will be given his due. The field of psychoanalysis will also be pressured, with understandings of subjectivity drawn from philosophers, novelists, poets, and musicians, from the vantage of their creative dilemmas and inhibitions. This approach not only places psychoanalysis in the world of others but also opens psychoanalytic views to its own potential literary education. Education, then, will serve as the fragile bond and the transitional space. There, in its various guises and in confrontation with art, education will lead us to the problem of learning to live from conflicts among love, hate, and ambivalence, affects of great force and persuasion needed to think. Affects without their symbolization are also where thought collapses, since they entangle need, demand, and desire with a terrible absence. Our greatest pedagogical theme will then collapse with the question of affect and from this ruin we will consider the urge toward reparation.

I have mentioned a few times, the conception of education, the thought of education, and thinking education. These conditions and points of vulnerability all turn on the question of emotional pain. Bion (1993a) understands thinking to be secondary to the advent of thoughts and, as noted earlier, he considered thoughts without a thinker from the vantage of "wild thoughts." He also believes this problem is insolvable and thus can only be met with care, humility, and curiosity. In Bion's view, thinking contains the emotional pain of thoughts, but also is the means for tolerating affect. Bion classified thoughts into three areas: preconceptions, or innate ideas, conceptions, or the linking of preconceptions to a realization or satisfaction, and concepts, having to do with a greater freedom of symbol formation. Concepts open elaboration, metaphor, reverie, and creativity. They come after. On this view thoughts impose themselves on the mind and thinking is the apparatus for digesting thoughts. "I repeat," Bion writes, "thinking has to be called into existence to cope with thoughts" (111). Bion sees thoughts as akin to the frustration of trying to know something unknown at the precise point where one must also encounter absence. The choice is stark: one either thinks thoughts or evacuates them.

Along with Arendt's (1993a) understanding of natality, thinking, and responsibility, the philosopher of modern critical theory, Theodor Adorno, who wrote on art, philosophy, and music, will be used as counterpoints to psychoanalytic views. Both wrote passionately about education and its responsibility. Like Arendt, Adorno (1998) writes with force about the destruction left in the wake of the evacuation of frustration: when the human destroys her or his own capacity to think humanely and exchanges this vulnerability for instrumental reason. Adorno, however, never spoke of infant development. He never noted, for instance, what the infant or child needed from others to become a proper human. Except for his letters to friends and family and his recently published dreams, Adorno rarely spoke of parents—the mother and father's love, or the son's disappointments and fears. Yet Adorno was concerned, even obsessed, with the problem of uneven development and our tendency toward regression to an archaic state: not of infancy, for the infant cannot know its own duration and, as Arendt saw it, infancy represents both our beginnings and reception into an already made world of others. In her sense, the infant is the original stranger and the question is whether adults could tolerate the vulnerable nature of this being.

Adorno's notion of what we could call backward development leaned on the psychoanalytic idea of thoughtlessness, a terrible identification with and projection of the destruction of the death drive. The regression he spoke of was cultural and found its home in education: that whole societies could enact a horror of the other, regressing to what he saw as an archaic state of superstition, then murderous rampage in the name of totalitarianism and fascism. The human, he insisted, was subject to inhumanity. Adorno's (1998) picture of development then begins with the devastating occurrence of adult regression—not to an earlier state—but to a terrible aggression where nothing would matter. And while he made this argument in many of his essays, his most devastating critique came under the title, "Education after Auschwitz." And this will lead him to pressure education: "The premier demand upon all education is that Auschwitz not happen again" (191). The essay drew from Freud's (1930/1929) *Civilization and Its Discontents* with the view that the speakable and the unspeakable go hand in hand and that it is the responsibility of education to symbolize these conflicts rather than repeat them.

While these philosophers saw the world in education, the psychoanalysts saw in the internal world something unworldly. Bion gave his attention to the paradox of internal frustration—whether it is tolerated or evaded and as that which ushers in the need to think and the force that destroys thinking. He owes a great deal to the theories of Melanie Klein who saw frustration, or what she called "phantasies," as conveying an original anxiety and defenses against this as the reason for why thinking is associated with mental pain. While Klein's views are discussed more fully in chapters three, four, and seven, her understanding of the relation between the infant and mother as the basis of psychical life, and so of object relations carried on and elaborated throughout one's life, are introduced here to raise startling questions of what it feels like to think at all.

Klein's (1937) turn to the infant, she maintained, was one way for her to "study the interaction of all the various forces which go to build up this most complex of all human emotions which we call love" (57). The mother is the first object of the infant's love and hate and Klein believed that the infant's urge for love is first felt through the bodily experience of satisfaction from the breast and that this experience begins the infant's capacity for phantasies of goodness. Phantasies of badness are made when the infant feels the mother's absence: no breast. This anxiety is the infant's reality and these phantasies feel as if they make the world, even as this anxiety fragments the world into bits and pieces. Klein (1937) simply termed this ongoing struggle as "the emotional situation of the baby" (58).

Klein's (1952) later description of what is emotional about this emotional world is vivid and shocking, specifically when she imagines the raging infant caught in its own riotous phantasies of frustration and hatred:

> In his destructive phantasies he bites and tears up the breast, devours it, annihilates it; and he feels that the breast will attack him in the same way. As urethral- and anal-sadistic impulses gain in strength, the infant in his mind attacks the breast with poisonous urine and explosive faeces, and therefore

expects it to be poisonous and explosive toward him. The details of his sadistic phantasies determine the content of his fear of internal and external persecutors, primarily of the retaliating (bad) breast. (63)

Klein believed these first horrific impressions of the infant were permanent, in the sense that our human situation is always emotional, that it mirrors our bodily helpless, which feels persecutory, and that it is absolutely beholden to the other's love. So original is the force of conflicts between goodness and love, and badness and hate, that they compose the internal world and set it to work with phantasies of destruction, anxieties over loss of love, archaic defenses against pain, and feelings of guilt and gratitude. Almost inexplicably—from such remorse and anguish, from a constitutive negativity—a desire for reparation will emerge. Klein will see this movement as the depressive position and the form it will take is symbolization, the gradual capacity to differentiate phantasy from the whole object. But because symbolization leans on absence, every perception, every blink of the eye, will pose the question of mourning or melancholia. Tolerating the emotional pain of existence will usher in the depressive position: feelings of pining, sadness, and loss joined with desires for love, reparation, and gratitude.

Yet before symbolization there is the power of bodily affect and what absence feels like. Joan Riviere (1964) put such feelings into memorable words:

> The baby cannot distinguish between 'me' and 'not-me'; his own sensations are his world, the world to him; so when he is cold, hungry or lonely there is no milk, no well-being or pleasure in the world—the valuable things in life have vanished. And when he is tortured with desire or anger, with uncontrollable, suffocating screaming, and painful, burning evacuations, the whole of his world is one of suffering; it is scalded, torn and racked too. . . . It is our first experience of something like death, a recognition of the non-existence of something, of an overwhelming loss, both in ourselves and in others, as it seems. And this experience brings an *awareness of love* (in the form of desire), and a *recognition of dependence* (in the form of need), at the same moment as, and inextricably bound up with, feelings and uncontrollable sensations of pain and threatened destruction within and without. (9)

From these bodily affects, both Klein and Riviere brought to our consideration a genealogy of love and an understanding that to love is to come into existence.

While Klein (1930) will speak a great deal about tolerating the actual world, in her discussion of the work of symbol formation, she considered these early phantasies of destruction and reparation as the means for developing a sense of reality: "As the ego develops, a true relation to reality is gradually established out of this unreal reality. . . . A sufficient quantity of anxiety is the necessary basis for an abundance of symbol-formation and of phantasy; an adequate capacity on the part of the ego to tolerate anxiety is essential if anxiety is to be satisfactorily worked over" (221).

The paradox Klein presents the baby with is that to encounter reality there must first be something that is not reality. Reality goes on without us, is painful to encounter, and, in this sense, may be linked to an original absence. To approximate any meaning will be to know one's emotional relation to reality and to retroactively symbolize that encounter. Yet this work depends on phantasies that also set meanings loose from the confines of the thing. These procedures are a part of reality itself since reality never stays the same and, if it does, then there is no reality at all. And so a great deal of the ego's work will be a working through or tolerating both the loss of the world as it wished it to be and feeling the anxiety that signals absence and the ego defenses. In Klein's view, and in much of what follows from it, thinking will be conceptualized as the creative transformation of affect into symbolization. And symbolization, or putting things into words, will be our greatest substitute for the original object and thus our most enigmatic resource.

The work of Klein and Bion on the emotional meaning and poetics of thinking thoughts and the understanding that thinking involves emotional pain revised Freud's view of how we come to think at all. Freud (1911) thought of this conflict through the divisions made between pleasure and reality. In his "Formulations on Two Principles of Mental Functioning" Freud described our earliest attempts to think our thoughts through primary and secondary processes made from the movements of pleasure and unpleasure and an encounter with what he called the reality principle. The large question for Freud concerned the action of "turning away from reality" (218), but also how we come to know the world and judge the difference between experience and event if thinking begins within the primary processes, or the "[Lust–Unlust] principle . . . the pleasure principle" (219). At the origin of thought, Freud placed a wish for pleasure into a hallucination of satisfaction. This wish is inevitably disappointed, and so another method will be used to form what Freud called a conception of the world beyond the wish. The baby will cry out for the other. In the name of pleasure, bodily action will then be the next attempt to affect one's world. The conflict between phantasy or hallucination and the need for satisfaction will set in motion a new principle: "what was presented in the mind was no longer what was agreeable but what was real, even if it happened to be disagreeable. This setting-up of the *reality principle* proved to be a momentous step" (219). What is momentous is that consciousness of the world comes into being from the wish for this world, a wish that is in some way a defense against what Freud called "motor discharge" (221) or the bodily force of affect: cries, screams, kicking, pushing away, and clinging, but also holding, grabbing, listening, and looking. These bodily actions that insist on presence are eventually, through symbol formation, transformed into what is most abstract about us: thinking thoughts and accepting psychical reality as an enigmatic wish to communicate without knowing what this communication brings. Thinking is how the body tolerates its needs, wants, and desires; it is the means for symbolizing absence and refinding the lost object.

When Freud placed the conflict between pleasure and reality principles as the basis of mental functioning, he made a relation to a nonrelation, and so kept thinking close to the *as if* world of imagination. His description of thinking says as much: thinking as "an experimental kind of acting" (221). What comes before this experiment, however, is its combustible material: the loss of the object, anxiety, hallucination, bodily affect, and doubts over ever refinding that first experience of satisfaction and bliss. As a part of the same mental process, thinking and phantasizing become "our weak spot" (223) because both emerge from anxiety over loss of the object, touching unpleasure and cueing the ego defenses. The eventual conflict that thinking will catch itself in is this: "Just as the pleasure-ego can do nothing but wish, work for a yield of pleasure, and avoid unpleasure, so the reality-ego need do nothing but strive for what is useful and guard itself against damage" (223). The perpetual trouble, however, is that what is useful and what incurs damage cannot be known in advance, that reason itself will be on the side of ego defenses and the negation of them, and that the reality ego will always experience uncertainty over meaning as it tries to refind its lost objects. Thinking, then, will never be so far way from the absence that calls it forth.

One curious turn concludes Freud's essay on these two mental principles and, in my view, interferes with the essay's circuitous meanings and Freud's thinking about thinking. He leaves his study of the internal world to comment on the conflict between art and education, as if to say the same dynamics of interiority repeat in the objects of perception, in our creative work, in our knowledge procedures, and in the institutions we place into the external world. Yet the repetition is never the same since our own self-difference cannot be completed by what we put into the world. With this idea of repetition, Freud's narrative style breaks into a list that introduces otherness into the heart of the reality principle: sexuality, neurosis, and the unconscious. The unconscious will be the scene of all havoc, affecting even the work of writing it into a sentence:

> (8) The strangest characteristic of unconscious (repressed) processes, to which no investigator can become accustomed without the exercise of great self discipline, is due to their entire disregard of reality-testing; they equate reality of thought with external actuality, and wishes with their fulfill-ment—with the event—just as happens automatically under the dominance of the ancient pleasure principle. (225)

So measures of reality suffer from symbolic equation, leading Freud to remark on the nature of the inquiry: "One is bound to employ the currency that is in use in the country one is exploring—in our case, neurotic currency" (225). Just as the very thought of education is about to enter Freud's essay, he seems to imply that to explore the nature of our reality we must use its neurotic currency to exchange it with something better, an education that no longer needs its neurotica.

Freud will place art on the side of the pleasure principle; it need not obey any rules of reality and so frees itself to create possibility. Yet he will also insist that art does something with the reality principle that makes it pleasurable since the artist's phantasies "are molded into truths of a new kind . . . as precious reflections of reality" (224). Education does not have this flexibility and Freud places it on the side of attempting to instill the real-ity principle. Yet, in so doing, education creates for itself a new contradic-tion because of how the reality principle comes to be a principle at all. While education tries to side with reality, what brings the reality principle to our side is the promise of refinding love, which then disturbs our perception of reality. Freud left us a clue as to a constitutive impossibility of education, a kernel of which will disorient education and become caught in the throat of an impossible profession:

> *Education* can be described without more ado as an incitement to the con-quest of the pleasure principle, and to its replacement by the reality prin-ciple; it seeks, that is, to lend its help to the developmental process which affects the ego. To this end it makes use of an offer of love as a reward from the educators; and it therefore fails if a spoilt child thinks that it possesses that love in any case and cannot lose it whatever happens. (224)

The problem is that education is not a conquest of reality but only a fragile tie to the uncertainties reality entails. It cannot proceed without the transference love, yet its procedures are vulnerable to the educator's pleasure principle, the countertransference.

Freud, Klein, and Bion leave us with the great problem of what it can mean to think at all and whether education is a solution or a problem. Each will bind thinking to a frustration, a wish, a lost object, and an object relation. Adorno will remind us of the traumatic collapse and art will serve as our radical hope. Each will suggest that thinking is a working through of that which resists yet is in need of symbolization in order to think. Love and hate will never be so far away, nor will our wishes to do away with the mental pain incurred from trying to know what can bring satisfaction. But without the wish to know, there will be no thinking at all. These are also the dilemmas made from education's offer of love. It cannot be unconditional because love is vulnerable to education and to the transference that makes it absurd. All that education has to give is the offer of the transference (Kohon 2005). The wish to know will also be where the pedagogical theme will collapse. As for the educator's paradox, it begins in a confusion of time. The educator was once a child with frustrated thoughts and fears over loss of love and is now in the position to frustrate others with an offer of love that cannot really be given without incurring loss, anxiety, defenses, and phantasies. Could it be that education, like psychoanalysis, is an attempt to cure by love?

LINES OF INQUIRY

In the chapters that follow, education will have a psychic life through transference and countertransference and a social life with its impossible insistence on adapting to reality. Sometimes education will appear as instituted education: schools, training institutes, and pedagogical exchange. At other times, education will take shape between the play of mothers and infants, where both will be subject to a future they cannot know but nonetheless, in their different ways, anticipate and act upon. The strangest education will take place in the psychoanalytic session: as catharsis, as mystery, as transference and countertransference, and as a love of language. The education we cannot know but that nonetheless insists will be associated with the unconscious. This will be our most accidental education and will contain resistance to learning. We will see education struggle with its unnameable qualities; times when what is unspeakable within its procedures destroys its promise for a future and leaves in its wake a terrible betrayal. This "bad education" will certainly be the problem in chapter three, a meditation on reading a novel, where education itself contains a phantasy of murdering its students, and where teachers resign themselves to their passion for ignorance, to not wanting to know anything about it.

We will also see that education is affected by the desire of the educator, yet this presents a problem for how we come to know our educational acts as distinct from and in conflict with the wishes they presuppose. Chapter five will consider this dilemma through the psychoanalytic concept of the countertransference and the problem will be reformulated in chapter seven with a focus on the status of conflict in learning the impossible professions. In both chapters, responsibility becomes caught in cycles of blame, guilt, and anxiety over fault and accountability. We will also see that the educator is a figure of learning as much as she or he symbolizes the procedures of knowledge. Here is where psychoanalysis enters with its question of where responsibility begins and how it comes about, taking as its focus the capacity, interest, and resistance created within the relationship between psychical life and the actual world. We will ask: what does our capacity for symbolization mean for recognition and self-understanding? The ways in which understanding the self and the world come about in this scene compose our first difficulty: we feel before we learn and affect carries a desire for its own truth, following the logic of the pleasure/unpleasure binary. Uneven development is the concern of chapter two, where the focus is on the education of teachers.

Thinking within psychoanalysis, just as thinking the thought of education, begins with the problem of resistance, or turning away. We have glimpsed why the thought of education is difficult to think, but now need to ask how psychoanalysis, as well, may appear as "a thought without a thinker." Four obstacles to thinking psychoanalytically in any education will illustrate the problem. The most obvious one is that psychoanalysis is actively avoided, even in psychoanalytic institutes. We will see how these avoidances constitute a commentary on the limits of our preconceptions of education as opposed to characterizing the problem of whether there can be a psychoanalytic conception of education that can analyze its own unfolding.

A second obstacle is intimate and has to do with what it can mean to represent the emotional force of education: what it feels like, the avalanche of worries involved, the sudden responsibilities entailed, and the convoluted relations that teachers and students and analysts and analysands find themselves entangled in and at times defeated by. Any attempt made to stabilize the object and the subject can be considered as a defense against the registration of difference that education brings and that psychoanalysis must posit (Bass 2000). The irony psychoanalysis proposes is that its words at once acknowledge our erotic ties—through the psychoanalytic terms of the transference, identification, and empathy, for example—and sensitize our need to resist them. Yet our terms for understanding cannot be known once and for all and this means that psychoanalysis as well is subject to its own unknown. Our third obstacle to psychoanalysis is internal. It involves the double idea that language itself may act therapeutically and that it may also collapse into a concreteness that forecloses the difference needed for the capacity to think. Some of these dilemmas are discussed in chapter six, through Freud's work with artists during times of war when the body censors words and so turns into inhibition in creativity: writer's block, arm paralysis, and stage fright.

Our fourth obstacle: psychoanalysis itself poses the greatest difficulty to thinking psychoanalytically. It founders on its own collapse of the pedagogical theme. We glimpsed the internal resistance of psychoanalysts to their own knowledge through Anna Freud's psychoanalytic education, when her teachers felt they needed to look down on her beginnings and where no matter how she expressed her interests, her teachers could only hear a child speak. This internal resistance to psychoanalysis forms the backdrop of chapter seven in which the drama of learning an impossible profession is staged and the question raised is whether any education can analyze is own unfolding.

Neither psychoanalysis nor education can come into being without their respective obstacles and conflicts and thus without our divided self. And nowhere is the problem of learning, thinking, and teaching more compellingly addressed than in psychoanalytic thought, specifically from the vantage of its clinical work and the questions that follow from it. How does a theory of learning become an experiment in therapeutics? Two lines of inquiry emerge from this question. In terms of the clinic, how does psychoanalytic theory affect its own practices and the analyst's conceptualization of the work? The interminable problem is whether the uniqueness of the psychoanalytic encounter can be maintained to affect its theories of the mind, the theorist's mind, and the transference of theory. The tension resides in the anxieties of theory and practice, how this conflict is symbolized, and whether the defense of splitting them into opposing forces continues to require us to take one side only to destroy our need for both. Just as our theories of life posit the difference among our actions in the world, our wishes for meaning, and what becomes of them, theory is that which pokes a hole in experience. Practice is not immune. It pokes a hole in itself through its own knowledge procedures, through what is unknowable in the truth it attempts to put into place. What is left is the hope that words matter. They promise a gap between the symbol and the thing and may betray that promise of containing the unknown. Words serve as a substitute for what cannot be present, yet nonetheless their own force must remind us of absence. But how do words matter to their own theory? Chapter three is a story of words that act like copycats. Chapter four describes this problem from the vantage of learning psychology in the midst of a collapse of the pedagogic theme.

Whereas our first line of inquiry concerns what could be called the psychic life of education from the vantage of its logic of affect and the phantasies that represent it, a second line will follow the psychoanalytic clinic into the clinic of education. We will see how the language of clinical psychoanalysis lends a hand to clarifying what our minds make of learning from the vantage of the impossible professions. Psychoanalytic narratives link education to the beginning of life, when communication promises satisfaction before understanding. This attuned mistiming, what may later be thought of as needed accidents, is continued throughout life; such uncertainty may have lead Freud to his paradoxical formulation of education as one of the impossible professions. These professions have a common interminability—their education. They will always be needed and this need for them will constitute and be constitutive of the radical incompleteness in their practices and theories.

The idea that a profession is impossible proposes to link the limits of practice to the complexity and uncertainty of its subjects. After all, the human professions have as their object others who are subjects. It is an intersubjective world we cannot know in advance of its event since its qualities are unstable, unrepeatable, and capable of movement, transformation, fixation, and regression. These professions are subject to both their own mind and to the minds of others that they cannot read. They are subject to their own secret thinking and to thoughts without a thinker. The reason these different histories of learning render these professions so impossible is that their theories and practices repeat the very difficulties of the subject/object divide made from the principles of mental functioning. If we stay close to Freud's admission of the impossible professions, we can also bring into this formulation problems within the education of the professions. What may be most impossible is the education of the impossible professions, particularly as the transference to education, because those who carry out the education of others convey both the experience of their own education and their experience of what is impossible in the profession itself.

What happens when we approach an education we have already had and the one not yet experienced as composing a quality of the impossible professions? Lacan's (1998a) formulation of the impossible posits a gap between demand and desire. Whereas when one makes a demand it appears to have its own object (namely, the other's attention), the field of desire is atmospheric, without an object. Desire, then, is only the desire to desire, yet without this desire the subject turns itself into an object. Consequently, impossibility is both an event and its limit. As an event, impossibility signifies the meeting of two dimensions of knowledge—the thing and its signification—that neither overlap nor attain identity with itself. Impossibility signifies a lack in the subject. We will consider this lack in chapter seven from the vantage of learning the impossible professions and how the subjective encounter with the event and the limit may open degrees of doubt and the space of creativity. In Lacan's view, only through doubting our existence can we begin to grapple with what it can mean to be a subject who is subjected to forces one cannot know in advance yet who attempts to anticipate what has not yet happened. The subject is that gathering point for all these unknowns that affect its constitution and lead to its strange pathways of desire. And Lacan will then place impossibility in the realm of love and knowledge. When Lacan (2006a) defined love as giving what one does not have to someone who does not want it, he placed lack and misrecognition at the heart of human desire. One of the most difficult dilemmas for education will concern how to think the collapse of this pedagogical theme of love as a feature of the work.

That love and education sound uncannily alike should give the reader some pause, as this returns the transference. From the beginning of its own "analytic infancy," psychoanalysis, too, entangles love with therapy. Freud (1974) admitted as much in a letter to Jung when he accepted the trouble that psychoanalysis was "the cure by love" (13). This was Freud's beginning attempt to index the ineffable qualities of need, demand, and desire that constitute and are constitutive of the transference, the key means for the psychoanalytic object relation to unfold, to stall, and to frustrate. Within this paradoxical hope, which we give to ourselves in both our symptoms and its cure, we can begin to think differently about the education of the impossible professions and how it is that the vicissitudes of love and hate are also their fate. While this transference is perhaps the most difficult reason for our troubles made in thinking the thought of education, without the transference, there can be no learning. The problem is whether education can become the means to create transference to words.

It may be useful to overview the chapters that follow in the order the reader will find them. Throughout the chapters, education will be separated from its own demand for order and compliance and will be brought closer to the things that were never meant to be education, but nonetheless become its responsibility. Because we cannot give reasons for our reasons and because reasons are not what cause our dilemma, our best approach will be to read between the lines and even read what is not there at all. Our cast of characters will be drawn from art, literature, philosophy, psychoanalysis, education, and life; we will follow the lines of their own pedagogic themes into collapse and then follow the urge for reparation.

Chapter two has, as its home, a field called education and the conflict known as teacher education. Teacher education usually refers to newcomers to the profession of teaching in compulsory settings, although its definition will be stretched to anyone encountering the pedagogical field. I introduce a notion of uneven development as other to the chronology of immaturity to maturity and inexperience to experience. This will open fundamental phantasies of development brought to the education of teachers and cultivated by this education. Such an approach will take us into problems of love and hate in learning and something unspeakable: that teachers may hate their education. I propose development as uneven and subject to regression, hatred, and not learning from experience. Development can then be understood as a problem of trying to know the mind that resists being known, to responsibility for the other, and as capable of containing frustration, or experience, provided that others can help us overcome what Bion (1994a) simply called, in his discussion of group experience, "a hatred of learning from experience" (86). We will see this formulation as agonizing the mantra of teacher education, namely, that we learn by experience. To posit a hatred of development as one of its constitutive features means that teacher education will have to find a way to work through its idealization of development, love, and experience. It will have to tell a new story of love and hate if its participants are to work through the old myths of the ultruistic, sacrificing teacher who cannot wait to teach and learn. To make this argument, I juxtapose three views of development that center the question of uncertainty and unevenness: William James, the psychologist who focused on the wandering mind, Arendt, the philosopher who focused on responsibility for a world one has not made, and Bion, the psychoanalyst who focused on what is unknown and maybe hated in affective relationships. Their views leave us with a way to think an ethics of teacher education in the postmodern university.

Chapter three tells the Kleinian story of reading Ishiguro's (2005) novel of education, *Never Let Me Go*. It is also a story of reading itself from the vantage of what we can learn about our own anxieties made from reading into illegible experience. One of the paradoxes of the reader is that she can read the words without knowing what they signify. Ishiguro's title itself is also used to refer to what education feels like. One problem in this chapter is that for the novel's characters there seems to be no fact of natality and so the impossible quest for their origin becomes unspeakable. The other problem proposes excess to reading between the lines. Chapter three introduces Klein's understanding of the act of reading under the supposition that a novel can teach us about our act of reading. Ishiguro's novel is analyzed as an occasion for thinking about reading as an allegory of psychic development. Drawing on the work of Klein and Arendt, my psychoanalytic reading explores the discord between the signifier and the signified, seeing this conflict as belonging to language, development, and social thought. I analyze the slow events of reading to illustrate two irresolvable conflicts animated and transferred onto the scene of reading: encountering what is illegible yet impressive in psychical reality and putting these impressions into language to speak and write about what is ambiguous and unknown in external reality. I suggest this novel of education may be read as a commentary on the internal world of object relations and its practices of reading, where Ishiguro's characters stand for, as they affect, our affective representations.

Readers meet Kleinian views again in chapter four, through an analysis of learning psychology from the side of its debates on the nature of existence. The experience of learning psychology will take two directions, themselves pressuring our pedagogical theme. From the knowledge procedures of a field called psychology there will be the problem of trying to convey this knowledge pedagogically through the lecture. What is it about trying to represent the mind that makes us nervous? From the phantasy procedures of our own psychology there will be a conflict in getting to know our phantasies of psychology. These two directions are rooted in an earlier history of reading that begins with being written upon by the other—our first psychology—and this chapter revolves around the idea that psychology makes us nervous because it takes a psychology to make a psychology, a human condition that gives to us our anxiety and our hope for goodness. Yet the history of the field of psychology forgets this dilemma by reducing our minds to behavior, consciousness, biology, and to the gray matter of neurons and their short circuits. In so doing, the field of psychology cannot think the question of what it can mean for a theory of learning to ponder the gray matter of our own insides, or what it can mean to exist in our psychological existence.

Chapter four brings psychology into the matter of gray existence. The collapse of this pedagogical theme will be approached with lectures on psychology given by Freud, Winnicott, and Adorno. Of different emphasis and style, each lecturer grappled with conveying the relation between the emotional world and the material world. All of them were more than aware of meeting an audience they would also attempt to create. To grasp what our poetics of existence can feel like, I then turn these other gray matters over to literature, by way of the literary genre of the *Zeitroman*, novels of disillusionment, critical of their own age. These are novels in which our protagonists cannot be in charge of themselves, yet are charged with the problem of the desire to know. Two novels of illness then take the stage as we meet our protagonists learning to think their thoughts through the crisis of love and hate. Klein (1946) thought of tolerating this crisis as the depressive position, a different quality of education that can accept its limits without splitting hated parts of the self into a disposed other. Returning again to this crisis of education, which is now posed as a crisis of subjectivity, I suggest two ways to conceptualize a theory of learning the impossible professions. One is through Klein's view of the depressive position, where she ties the question of thinking to the capacity to mourn the losses development and learning leave in their wake. The second draws upon Lear's (2006) study of radical hope, where a radical reconceptualization of existence depends on the hope for something good, even as one cannot know in advance where such thinking may lead.

Both Klein and Lear begin with scenes of devastation: for Klein, the devastation is constitutive of internal processes made from anxiety and for Lear, the devastation is the loss of cultural life and every meaning that gives this life value and beauty. While their contexts are utterly different and without comparison, both suggest that the human cannot prepare for its destructions and traumas. Learning, as radical reformulation of what it can mean to live emerges in the afterward of devastation. I believe this orientation to learning made from the urge for reparation and radical hope would well serve our thinking the frustrated thought of education—indeed, could be put into the service of tolerating the mental pain incurred by the very thought of education. Along with the work of Klein, I propose that the work of thinking the thought of education permits education an encounter with its own depressive position.

Problems of learning the impossible profession structure chapter five, where the teacher and the analyst confront what education can mean if we understand the paradoxes of education, not from the procedures of its knowledge and claims of truth but through the ineffable love and hate conveyed by the countertransference. I ask whether education can be a psychoanalytic education and thus whether it is possible for an analysis of education's own unfolding. We will see how the act of understanding the emotional world of the teacher and the analyst through the psychoanalytic concept of the countertransference leads us into debates on the status of both education and the countertransference. While Anna Freud (1995) tried to divide the work of education and psychoanalysis with the idea that "something more besides analysis is required to undo [ego defenses]. The child must learn to tolerate larger and larger quantities of unpleasure without immediately having recourse to his defense mechanisms . . . [and] theoretically it is the business of education rather than of analysis to teach him this lesson" (64–65), we will see that the business of education puts into place anxiety and defense that are conveyed through the teacher's countertransference. I suggest that countertransference to education is composed from the analyst's and teacher's affective history of education and when the teacher or analyst considers her or his emotional world, she or he confronts something that cannot be experienced, that is, what education disavows and so what was never imagined as important to interpreting our learning—namely, our helplessness, frustration, and anxiety.

The transference returns in chapter six, through the strangers I call "transference people," my misreading of a discussion on transference that leads me to a focus on the problem of interpreting a history that is unforgivable with the antidepressant of narrative. A number of contexts are brought together: Freud's analysis of the poet H.D., her self-analysis made after she left Freud, and understanding my transference to this history during a trip I made to Germany. The chapter is an attempt at repairing a collapse of pedagogical themes with an effort to hold the present in mind even as the past has its own annihilating pull. This tension is also found within Freud's analysis with artists. H.D. was suffering from an inhibition of creativity with feelings of a wrecked life choked with strangulated words. Here we will see psychoanalysis as an invitation to write one's own novel with the gamble of what creativity must risk: the translation of affect into symbols. In 1933, H.D. traveled to Vienna to undergo an analysis with Freud. She was not the first artist Freud analyzed, but was his last one and his most eloquent advocate. Other artists who contacted Freud because of their inhibitions of life's creativity are also discussed to raise a significant dilemma for contemporary education. This psychoanalysis will lead us to consider that if part of the work of education is trying to know one's own pedagogical themes, including where they may collapse into despair, another part of this responsibility turns on an interest in the work of enlivening what may feel like the dead objects within the internal world. The chapter also becomes an occasion for thinking through what it meant for H.D. and Freud to have worked together through the rise of National Socialism and how one analysis thus came to address the actual world of terror by regarding the subject, by seeing words as important at a time when words and people were being destroyed. From this difficult knowledge, I raise some questions this devastating history has left us to think. What was never meant to be education is precisely the responsibility education inherits.

Chapter seven returns the question of thinking the very thought of education through Freud's idea of "the impossible professions," with the speculation that the Achilles' heel of the impossible professions is their own education. So many impossibilities are lost and found in this work: the transference, the subject presumed to know, anxiety and inhibitions, and the work of the impossible in itself. We will stretch Freud's formulation of the impossible professions to the theater of subjectivity and then, again, to a matter that Lear (2006) raised as "radical hope," a hope that changes the very nature of hope. We will see again that education, as much as it is a form of thought and a structure of knowledge procedures, competes with that which is not education at all, namely, narcissism and emotional storms. Indeed, the figure that will bear this burden of transference is the phantasy Lacan (1998b) called "the subject who is supposed to know" (230). This last chapter turns on the difficulty of understanding why, all too often, the thought of education dissolves into anxieties of really bad pedagogy and therefore gives away our capacity to think the collapse of our pedagogical themes. If Freud's formulation of the impossible professions proposes a constitutive difficulty within our practices and theories and therefore teaches us something about the problems entailed when thinking the very thought of education, Bion's (2000) note on "making the best of a bad job" returns us to our prosaic encounters: a proposal to think the thought of education as our vulnerability, as a radical hope that changes the nature of hope itself, as a call to thinking the inevitable frustrations education brings, and as an ethic of trying to get to know our obstacles to encountering the unknown.

CHAPTER TWO

UNEVEN DEVELOPMENT

If we speak of development as a progression from immaturity to maturity, as a unifying property of the individual, and thus as capable of expression without conflict, we are apt to miss the fact of development as our human condition. We are likely to forget that all of us are subject to the radical uncertainty of being with others in common and uncommon history and that this being with other beings makes development uneven and uncertain. If we forget that development takes its own novel time, we are likely to become impatient with ourselves and with others. Yet development, too, carries its own traces of antidevelopment, areas of irresolvable conflict—incompleteness—that return as if it did not belong to itself, and to qualities of retroactive time that not only defer its meaning but provide the self with its new understandings of old events. The problem with development is that it is always on the move, even in moments of fixation given the defensive strategies needed to stay in a place that no longer exists. For Adorno (2006), we cannot speak of development without understanding its tendency toward regression. While Bion (1994a) will add to development its emotional collapse, the problem of hatred of development, Hans Loewald's (2000b) sense of development will have its revelatory qualities. And Arendt (1993b) will place development within the fact of natality, our beginnings as met by the reception from those already here. Still more: the psychologist of pragmatism, William James (1950), will track development as activity in perpetual movement and perhaps they will all agree that development is always uneven development.

As for the field of teacher education, by which I mean that place where those learning to teach confront knowledge about the development of others as they, too, develop their teaching selves, when theories of development are spoken there, we rarely begin with these enigmatic developments. Instituted education still manages to approach development as if it is a correction for childhood and its misadventures, as if development could cure its own unconscious wishes. Our inquiries have not thought the problem of our childhood's strange duration: how, even compulsively, when faced with new and familiar events, whatever our age, our time unconsciously repeats timeless conflicts. We may speak of development as an overcoming conflict, but not as conflict itself. We may agree that others develop, but rarely do we wonder how our own development affects our educational imagination and how this also affects its own development. Nor do we tend to think of development as composing and revising a history of learning to live with others and maybe feeling loneliness in this work. And we seem to miss the fact that our time of development is set by a strange clock, one that contains its own tendency to repeat, regress, and fixate on moments of breakdown or gratification. We assume that development in teacher education is unaffected by the social fact of having to be educated. However much our front-door discourses of teacher education seem to protect us from these unwieldy matters, remnants of our childhood slip in through the back door of our theories of teaching and learning. The work of this chapter is to consider areas of development in our field that remain conceptually underdeveloped and try to understand why this is the case.

Our opening problem is this: we have grown up in schools, have spent our childhood and adolescence observing teachers and our peers, and when we enter the field of teacher education, this avalanche of experience we have undergone, made from schooling, confirms itself (Britzman, 2003b; 2006). Growing up in education permeates our meanings of education and learning; it lends commotion to our anticipations for and judgments toward the self and our relations with others. It makes us suspicious of what we have not experienced and lends nostalgia to what has been missed. Simply put, our sense of self and our sense of the world are profoundly affected by having to grow up in school. And this means that both the experience we have and the having of experience are problems of education. As much as the field of teacher education represses this peculiar childhood of education, as much as those teaching in the university insist that teaching and learning are two different events, the repressed returns.

The great repression of teacher education returns as paradox: newcomers learning to teach enter teacher education looking backward on their years of school experience and project these memories and wishes into the present that they then identify with as somehow an indication of what should happen or never happen again. Teacher educators greet these newcomers as if they lack school experience and have no past. Both hold tight to deeply ingrained fantasies of education, repeating without remembering their childhoods through the idea of the teacher. They already know about good and bad students. Implicitly, the structure and ethos of teacher education gravitate toward our childhood view of education: this oddly resistant childhood is cast in cement with the mantra, "we learn from experience." So what can development actually mean when we cannot seem to leave our childhood of education? How is our field capable of changing itself, of developing responsibility for its representations, if everyone involved in teacher education was once a child who grew up in school and so relies on their infantile archive of education?

To look deeper into these quandaries, let us consider our beginnings through a radical claim, belonging to a psychoanalyst of development and environmental provision. Winnicott (1986a) proposed, "There is no such thing as an infant" (39). He did so to remind his colleagues that the infant comes with caregivers, and then toys and the transitional objects that make an infant into its own transitions. Our infancy is made as a relation to others. In this spirit, let us suppose there is no such thing as development, unless, of course, we can begin to conceptualize real and fantasized relationships, institutions, practices, culture, other minds, and education. There is no such thing as development unless we can begin thinking with what Winnicott (1987) called, in another context, "the fact of dependence" (83). If the question of development means there are always others because of the fact of dependence, then we cannot really think about development without also considering relations of responsibility and wonder about the conditions that would value the uncertainty of development as a strange and even alienating resource for understanding the great conflicts our field absorbs, creates, and lives within. Our study of development leads us far afield, into ongoing debates on the status of uncertainty in the impossible professions.

Our anxieties over essentialism have stalled our debates with the question of what should count as essential in the education of teachers. And it should not escape us that these conflicts over the basics mirror larger public anxieties over the education of children, youth, and university students and now the qualifications of teachers and university professors. It is an anxiety that conditions the scene of learning to teach: because schooling is a mass experience, because we humans have to have education, we are all experts at knowing what has been missed or what we should have had more of and we may be fairly insistent on knowing what works perfectly well and what we anticipate as going terribly wrong. In this schizoid world we become experts in lack. But this makes our expertise into a defense against all that is uncertain about our profession. We seem to experience amnesia here because if, in our early years, we once entered schools as frightened strangers and felt this new place as utterly strange, by the time we leave, we have turned ourselves into anthropological informants, experts with our own experience, eager to share and even impose this experience onto others. Somehow the having of school experience dulls our thinking. Somehow, the uncertainty that is our beginning has become predicable and routine. And somehow, we have forgotten our human condition as strangers, and that we are always, as Kristeva (1991) put it, "strangers to ourselves."

I think we come to the heart of the matter when we turn to the problem of existence. Many years ago, Maxine Greene (1973) named the teacher "as stranger." She proposed the teacher as an incomplete project, as unfinished, and as a searcher in the process of becoming a teacher with others. If the teacher chooses to become a critical subject, she supposed, what is critical only emerges when the teacher understands herself or himself as subject to uncertainty and as a subject with other subjects. And this uncertainty resides within the acts of a self, committed to its own becoming. The teacher has a choice to choose her past, to wake up, and to experiment: "the teacher who dares to do philosophy must be open to such a multiplicity of realities" (11). And unanswerable questions must be posed and dare I say enjoyed.

Greene imagined teacher education not through debates on proper preparation but as philosophy in the making, as dialogue with others, and as incomplete. There will always be work to do, but also, if we take the idea of multiple realities seriously, there will be conflict, new knowledge made, interpretations to doubt, and struggles with the question of truth. And the teacher's uncertainty will be both a disruption and a resource for hope. Greene's address to the teacher's learning, then, links freedom to courage: "If he can learn to do philosophy, he may liberate himself for understanding and choosing. He may liberate himself for reflective action as someone who knows who he is as a historical being, acting on his freedom, trying each day to be" (7). The teacher's unfinished work is to understand her representations of education as a project of learning to live with others. Existentially, development is uneven and uncertain because it is always affected by the question of freedom.

To analyze these existential dilemmas of learning to teach, I turn first to ideas from two philosophers who addressed, at different times and with different stakes, problems in conceptualizing development in teacher education: William James, whose psychology of teaching and learning ushered in the twentieth century and Arendt, whose philosophy of the crisis of education occurs in the midst of the twentieth century. Later, their concerns will be brought into tension with the stagnant situation Bion (1994a) called "the hatred of learning by experience" (86). His alienating assumption is that to understand the conflicts of development from the perspective that development means transformation, indeed, refers to what can feel catastrophic, one must explore the idea that there is also a hatred of development because development signifies loss and empty space. The chapter concludes with observations on our current context—the postmodern university—and the problem this untimely time leaves us to think when we think about our uncertain conditions in teacher education. For now, let the work of James and Arendt set the stage for understanding the fragility of our grand metanarratives in teacher education. Their work brings us to a problem beyond the childhood of education and that our childhood also presupposes, namely, development as uncertainty, as subject to the fact of dependency, and as an ongoing question of ethics and responsibility.

Readers may wonder what the pragmatist James and the critical theorist Arendt had in common. While both taught in the university and I believe considered themselves as teachers, for a brief moment in their long careers they shared an object of inquiry that neither of them prepared for, namely, the education of educators. Their collective concern is the teacher's responsibility for her and his own learning. Entry into discussions of this responsibility differed: for James, it was psychology and for Arendt, political thought; for James, it was the nature of the inner world, and for Arendt, the relation between adult and child; for James, education confronted the problem of instinctual life and for Arendt, education is lost and found in the world of others. Arendt proposed education as a problem of commitment and social responsibility and as animating and deadening relations of self and other. James entered the problem with his question of the teacher's passion and the difficulty of having one's own mind as one tries to influence others. Together, they outlined existential situations faced when the teacher chooses an education that is not yet present. Their sense of both psychology and social thought is neither solipsistic nor altruistic. In other words, these thinkers go beyond the great binary that catches short our educational imagination: whether teacher education should be focused on knowing oneself or dedicating one's life to others. Indeed, this schizoid divide forecloses the existential question the teacher confronts: what is it, in an impossible profession, to choose uncertainty?

A NEW RESPONSIBILITY

Around 1906, before there was something called teacher education, William James was invited to address the newly formed Department of Education at Harvard University. It was a heady time: the education of children was now linked to the university's responsibility for the education of teachers and the profession of education itself became tied, simultaneously, to the vicissitudes of compulsory schooling and the university. Already James (1950) was a famous psychologist, known for his two-volume work *The Principles of Psychology*, which outlined his orientation to understanding the nature of the human mind in relation to the interruptions and mysteries of life. So these principles relied on James's attempt to understand his own mind and all that interrupted it, including profound bouts with depression and writing blocks, with overcommitments, incapacity to finish projects, and inability to make a decision (Richardson 2006).

In James's view, understanding the human mind was the grand theme of and challenge to the new field of teacher education. And when he talked to teachers, he counseled that in trying to understand the human mind, there would be confusion and resistance to understanding. For example, James (1983) suggests, we might hold a mistaken view of childhood and render it so simple that we ourselves would see childhood as something to master, something one leaves behind. We might feel the child's mind as empty, as in need, and as something only to be instructed. We might take away the very mind we are trying to communicate with. And if that happens, James suggests, we lose our own minds as well, for, in James's view, the mind was never single-minded but in contact with other minds.

Trying to write about the mind was also a problem. In his lumbering two volumes on psychology, James (1950) felt that his topic—the idea that "thoughts and feelings exist and are vehicles of knowledge" (vi)—was almost impossible to write about without drowning in metaphysics and having to wrestle with the question of the soul. And there would be no end point. Additionally, the metaphysics of the soul can only gesture toward a radical uncertainty and the limits of knowledge. This problem concludes the first chapter of his *Principles* when James writes: "The boundary line of the mental is certainly vague" (6). James then advises readers to skip those few chapters that mire themselves in metaphysics. He warns his readers about what will happen to them as they begin a gigantic chapter in his second volume: "Chapter 20, on Space-perception, is a terrible thing" (v). And indeed he is right, at least to this reader, for the avalanche of material presented threatens to crash into a thousand tiny unruly thoughts and the reader may lose her way as James winds his way through the maze of the psychology of perception, sensation, and cognition. Without warning, James finds himself entangled in a philosophical debate: does the object world create understanding or does our mind create the world? Do we receive meaning from experience or does the meaning we make create what we represent as experience? Does language merely name reality or is reality a consequence of having language? That we want to know the nature of reality and our responsibility to it, he seems to imply, is why each of us has our own speculative psychology.

James's *Principles of Psychology* discusses such things as instinct, habits, attention, memory, association, apperception, and the will. Each quality of the mind is in conflict with its others, which led to his interest in specifying the design and force of mental acts. He wished to clarify what happens to perception when the human represents the world and what happens to the mind as we perceive the world. And he wondered how ideas affect the mind and how the mind affects or metabolizes ideas. Metaphysics are not far behind and this frustrates the pragmatist James. Perhaps he surprised himself when he wrote unanswerable questions: what is indelible about experience? What makes us human? And what is the nature of consciousness and its experience? He could not differentiate between our capacity to doubt the mind and our mind's creation of its own doubts. Can unanswerable questions, he wondered, matter to how we understand how the human learns?

James (1983) revised these cumbersome volumes when he brought his psychology to those learning to teach. In my view, he had the good sense to leave out chapter 20 and condense his meandering psychology into some short, passionate lectures. The book that resulted has a lovely title, *Talks to Teachers on Psychology and to Students on Some of Life's Ideals* and one really does get the sense that he is speaking to someone who is trying to learn a profession. His method was introspection, and he took the phenomenological approach. He will create the experience of the mind that he will then represent. He will posit the teacher's mind before there is a teacher. He will concern himself with the other and insist on the limits of our knowledge. He will posit a pedagogical orientation to his notion of mind and create new approaches to everyday problems. And he will present consciousness as continuous, as consciousness of something in both its dreamy inattention and its heightened, aroused states.

There is a background problem, not stated explicitly to his teacher audience, with the idea of consciousness as continuous. In a chapter titled "Attention" in *Principles of Psychology*, he gives us a clue of something discontinuous in consciousness and it has to do with a problem many teachers and professors have felt—the difficulty faced when having to write a lecture. James's description of his busy avoidance is timeless:

> One snatches at any and every passing pretext, no matter how trivial or external, to escape from the odiousness of the matter at hand. I know a person, for example, who will poke the fire, set chairs straight, pick dust-spects from the floor, arrange his table, snatch up the newspaper, take down any book which catches his eye, trim his nails, waste the morning *anyhow*, in short, and all without premeditation,—simply because the only thing he *ought* to attend to is the preparation of a noonday lesson in formal logic which he detests. Anything but *that*! (421)

One finds in his writing a capacity to enter the contents of his own mind, including what is most incoherent. At times, it is a dusty mind, a manic mind racing ahead without reason, obsessing over odd routines. Instead of writing a lecture, he will clean his house, write a letter, and imagine that setting the outside straight will inspire an internal housecleaning. But he will also wonder why time must be wasted, why the lecture is so difficult to write, and how the mind projects itself into the world to refind and perhaps contain its own confused contents. In this sense, if consciousness is continuous, it is also easily broken, not so much by the outside world but by that which it resists internally, namely, the unconscious. And, for James, this meant there really is a difficulty in knowing one's own mental acts, including its most disagreeable, chaotic ones.

James's big idea is that what is basic to the teacher's education is her or his understanding of what other people are like. People are not static entities waiting to be taught so that they can then learn in an orderly fashion. They are difficult to know because they have their own minds. Moreover, the mind works through the stream of consciousness, through association, and so it is always in motion and in relation to or chasing someone. The mind will not hold still and the body is not a separate thing waiting to take its instruction. This radical relationality, an intersubjectivity without permission, he said, will be an obstacle to education. For if attention is always fleeting attention, if attention occurs because of pleasure, the awareness of this psychology makes the teacher's work difficult. Still, the teacher's work develops from trying to learn what the student is like while attempting to interest her or his attention. Conflicts then are the heart of this relation and James (1983), ever the pragmatist, blasted away at the romance of what he called "a soft pedagogy":

We have of late been hearing much of the philosophy of tenderness in education;'interest' must be assiduously awakened in everything, difficulties must be smoothed away. Soft pædagogics have taken the place of the old steep and rocky path to learning. But from this lukewarm air the bracing oxygen of effort is left out. It is nonsense to suppose every step in education can be interesting. The fighting impulse must be appealed to. Make the pupil feel ashamed of being scared at fractions, of being 'downed' by the law of falling bodies; rouse his pugnacity and pride, and he will rush at the difficult places with a sort of inner wrath at himself that is one of his best moral faculties. (41–42)

At the heart of education James placed the problem of fear and asked the teacher to know how to use it. He was not afraid to suggest the need for the teacher's authority and the mobilization of the student's aggression in order to bite into new knowledge. He had the courage to destroy the teacher's illusion that somehow education will be a smooth affair if only the right technique could be applied. Interest, he seems to imply, is not something one begins with. But he also had the good sense to remind the teachers that education is not a funfair of instant gratification. And the mind that knows, he warns, resists being known. Indeed, the mind may not want to know even if it can know.

Perhaps his cautions allowed second thoughts about this "soft pedagogy" since he returns to reformulate it by considering the teacher's responsibility. He tries for some clarification: "Elicit interest from within, by the warmth with which you care for the topic yourself" (72). The problem, it turns out, is with the teacher's passion, with what the teacher cares about when the teacher cares about the student's interests. The mind, after all, is an intersubjective mind, not an ideal to achieve or a thing to fill with knowledge. Good night, Descartes: even as we need our own mind to know this, there is no mind without the other's mind. There is no passion without the other's passion. One more turn will be made. Near the end of these lectures, James will say that what makes life significant includes the capacity to accept insignificance or absence. So there are no promises for the future and there is no future without conflict, questions, and loss. Education, he implies, requires the courage for making ideas unhabitual. Education, he implies, defamiliarizes and even disrupts our suppositions. Education, we might say, makes us strangers, for there is nothing stranger and even estranging than trying to understand the other's mind while we make up our own.

Almost sixty years later, Arendt (1993b) would consider the teacher's education, not from the artistic problem of attitude, but from the social vantage of the crisis that education presents to both teachers and students. She joined the problem of education to larger cultural and historic changes still being worked through today. And she almost apologized for doing so, insisting that she entered the debate of education only as a philosopher-stranger, not as an educator. It is one of her strangest claims in that, while her view of education makes us all educators, actual teachers in compulsory settings are not considered, as Greene (1973) considered them, philosopher-strangers.

Arendt, too, considered the special characteristics of the child, but rather than specify psychological processes, as James did, she confronted the existential problem of having to be educated and the teacher's responsibility for this fact of dependency. She saw the child as a newcomer to the world, as a stranger to those already there. The child, a new human being, is in the process of becoming human. The child, in other words, begins with an uncertain relation to the world of others and to life itself. For Arendt, this meant that the teacher has a difficult responsibility: Teachers, because they greet children into the world they already live in, must take responsibility for the world that the child could not have made. Both must choose history. Arendt (1993b) puts the paradox boldly: "The teacher's qualification consists in knowing the world and being able to instruct others about it, but his authority rests on his assumption of responsibility for that world" (189). Like James, qualifications and authority are two different matters. Unlike James, there is a political problem. Teachers are responsible for the world they live in, even if by the fact of their natality they also entered the world they have not made. But by virtue of living in this world, by virtue of development, they make the world that greets their students and they are responsible for knowing about this world. The teacher's authority will be linked to knowing the world and taking responsibility for it. The responsibility is difficult, even painful, and it raises another dimension of dependency. Teachers are responsible for a world by choosing responsibility and so are dependent on both the world and on the new relation with the child. Neither qualification nor authority will tell one how this occurs. And so the teacher chooses both uncertainty and responsibility.

To understand the depth of this ethical quandary of authority as responsibility for the world they live in and have made by virtue of development, Arendt (1992b) turns to literature and quotes Shakespeare's *Hamlet*. Hamlet complained about existence as such when he said: "The time is out of joint. O cursed spite that ever I was born to set it right" (192). While James (1950, vol. II) as well would call on Hamlet's despair, in his *Principles*, his stress would be on the pleasure of completing a difficult task even if one wished to avoid it. For Arendt (1993b) there is no conclusion:

> Basically we are always educating for a world that is or is becoming out of joint, for this is the basic human situation, in which the world is created by mortal hands to serve mortals for a limited time as home. Because the world is made by mortals it wears out; and because it continually changes its inhabitants it runs the risk of becoming as mortal as they. (192)

Here is where the tragic and the potential meet. We are always educating for a world in crisis, a world that is a human world and so will, like the human, wear out. Those who renew the world are ones just entering it. Arendt's idea is that the essential relation of education is determined by what she calls our natality: that we are born and that others welcome us in our absolute dependency. Our mortality means that we are also responsible for making room for the new. Arendt is careful in what she supposes the teacher's work entails: teachers are obligated to tell the students what the world is like, not to instruct them in the art of living. It boils down to our attitude toward the fact of natality. And everything is at stake: "Education," Arendt (1993b) concludes, "is the point at which we decide whether we love the world enough to assume responsibility for it and by the same token save it from that ruin which, except for renewal, except for the coming of the new and young, would be inevitable" (196).

As you may hear in both James and Arendt, when it comes to education, what is essential is the crisis of education. The time of education is always out of joint because of the nature of the mind, because of the nature of the world, because of the nature of dependency, because of the asymmetry of authority, and because of the nature of responsibility. Many years later, Derrida (1994) will also ruminate on this problem of our out-of-joint time by attending to two of its disjunctions: that of injustice, as Hamlet sensed when he felt he was being asked to choose his becoming, and the one presented by the other, the disjunction of difference Derrida also called justice. Derrida, too, will speak of justice without condition, linking responsibility for the other to "hospitality without reserve" (65). The hospitality without reserve will take responsibility for the stranger.

There is no conclusion for responsibility because, as we try to find out where it leads, we confront the problem of love and ethics. And Arendt considers education as presenting a difficult choice between loving and hating the world, between the work of setting it right and the sadness incurred with the knowledge that the world wears out. I think this choice characterizes the existential condition of teacher education and raises the problem of a psychoanalytic pedagogy of uncertainty. We must now send the teacher back to school. Which choice did teacher educators face when they were children in schools? Did they have teachers who accepted responsibility for a world they did not make? Did their teachers love the fact of natality and so showed themselves unafraid of dependency, helplessness, and thus the unpredictability of life? Did their teachers wonder about what the child's mind was like? Or did their education wear out before its own time?

ON THE HATRED OF DEVELOPMENT

So far, I have been sketching an ethics of teacher development. With James and Arendt I have proposed the problem of teacher education as trying to understand and address the mind of the other and doing so in a way that the teacher is taking responsibility for both a mind she has not made and a world she is responsible for by virtue of development. With Greene, I have put the teacher into the position of the stranger, one who even by virtue of development is incomplete and searching. With the help of Winnicott, I have also described the concept of development from the vantage of its uneven and uncertain qualities because of its relation to our fact of dependency. And I have posed a paradox from which teacher education operates: that we grow up in school and that we return there as adults, that we bring to teacher education our own history of learning, only to meet the teacher educator's history of learning. To question whether all we can do is wear ourselves out, I now turn to a psychology of uncertainty unafraid of emotional pain. Unlike James, who saw consciousness as continuous, Bion insisted on the problem of discontinuity through the psychoanalytic idea of the unconscious. Existence as being is constituted through conflictive mental structures that cannot know its own representations but nonetheless represent its distortions and frustrations. And one form frustration can take is a hatred of development—one's own and those of others. Tying development to the problem of discontinuity means that there is something antidevelopmental about development, and this idea incurs a great deal of resistance since it goes against the idealization of development as progress and since it gets under the skin of this illusion to analyze how progress comes to be unconsciously equated with loss. Indeed, to bring into the discussion Bion's (1994b) concept of hatred of development may cause consternation and despair and agitate our most violent defenses.

We are approaching one of the reasons why the very thought of education becomes what Bion (1997) called "a thought without a thinker" (27). Education wears out not only because we are mortal but also because there is a hatred of learning from experience. And the way this hatred of development plays out in our field is through the terrible insistence that teachers hate their own teacher education. They convey their disgust to the newly arrived undergoing their own teacher education. Teachers may have hated the dependency that also characterizes learning to teach. They may have felt punished for their own uncertainty and so wish to protect others from what has already happened to them. They may have forgotten the fact of natality, or that they are responsible for a world they have made. Teachers may say to newcomers: "My teacher education was irrelevant, the real experience is here in my classroom, and theory is not useful." Teachers and student teachers may believe that the university idealizes theory and ignores practical constraints. They may wish for a theory without conflict, a perfect practice, and even compliant students. Yet all of these wishes are frustrated and this frustration is projected back into the field now as a hatred of theory, itself a derivative of development. Let me put the problem of what inhibits thinking the thought of education in a shocking idea: teacher education is a hated field and no one wants to be responsible for this bad education. Those in the university who may hate their own teaching hate it and those undergoing their teacher education meet this hate with their own hate. No teacher really loves her or his own teacher education. And university professors rarely identify their pedagogy as subject to their discontentment with having to learn. All may soften this rage by projecting it back into their own education with the vague complaint that "they didn't prepare me for the uncertainty."

What are we to make of this? Bion has argued that there is a hatred of development, a hatred of learning because learning, for the adult, means thinking about one's painful emotional experience of helplessness, dependency, and frustration. Bion (1994a) will name this frustration "experience," and all experience will be emotional experience, or trying to get to know something unknown and unknowable. In his discussion of experience in groups he will posit "a hatred of learning from experience" (86). Oddly, this hatred emerges from the need for security that scaffolds basic assumptions that protect the group from the insecurity of existence, that is, having to be with others. Keep in mind that Bion defines experience as frustration. Experience cannot be known in advance. While undergone, there is a kernel of unthinkability that incurs mental pain. In Bion's view, there are only two ways to deal with the frustration that uncertainty or not knowing creates. One can evacuate these feelings and consider the world of strangers as the source of distress. These evacuated feelings will destroy reality along with the group's capacity to think and to be open to new ideas. Yet new ideas mean the loss of old ones and so change feels catastrophic. The other way of experiencing frustration is to try to think about it, even if it means thinking about what one does not know. One thinks about frustration to modify, digest, and contain emotional experience. One learns with others to tolerate the frustration of having to learn from experience.

Then what is learning? For Bion, learning signifies at least two problems. Learning disrupts the old ideas and, if all goes well, allows for new ideas to be enjoyed. Learning is also an emotional acceptance of our ignorance because we do not really know what will happen with this new knowledge, nor will we be able to prepare for the destruction of the old knowledge. Here is where progress is unconsciously equated with loss. Learning means understanding that knowledge does not exhaust what is unknowable and that we act from not understanding. We may then become receptive to what has not been thought or understood without evacuating the uncertainty. Only then can responsibility emerge. Reality becomes larger, not smaller. Bion (1994b) defines learning this way:

> Learning depends on the capacity for the container [by which he means the capacity to hold doubt and not knowing without evacuating the bad feelings this involves] to remain integrated and yet lose rigidity. This is the foundation of the state of mind of the individual who can retain his knowledge and experience and yet be prepared to reconstrue past experiences in a manner that enables him to be receptive of a new idea. (93)

Provided that the past can be thought anew, learning may be understood as learning from emotional experience. If knowledge is to survive, then learning from experience must also become what Bion (1994b) calls "tolerance of doubt and tolerance of infinity" (94) or an acceptance of the unknown and the unknowable. And this makes strangers of us all. The defenses of splitting the world into good and bad can then be analyzed as the problem that destroys the mind's capacity to think. Thinking becomes more complicated, an experiment in responsibility for the unknown. Our responsibility is to interpret reality, and, in Arendt's terms, to try to tell others what our world is like.

Bion's interest in the hatred of development clashes with our commonsense understanding of experience as the royal road to learning, as meaning's punctuation, and as a cure for inexperience. It is noteworthy that Bion's understanding of development emerges from the study of group psychology, itself the foundation of education. The basic assumptions of groups, he suggests, begin with a desire for security as a defense against the unknown, but this means that insecurity, also a feature of individual and group life, will frustrate security. In teacher education, our security blanket of learning from experience actually creates profound insecurity, anxiety, and defense. The insecurity is expelled, only to return in the form of bad students, bad grades, bad theory, bad university, and bad methods. Persecution takes the place of responsibility. To consider these refusals as indicating a hatred of development, however, is not easily accepted since the teacher often supposes herself to be a motivator for the development of others. This idealization is a defense against the teacher's anxiety over her own development and all that is unknown in its making. In this sense, idealization may indicate fear of loss of love. And indeed, the hatred of development is that loss of love.

The large question presented concerns the idea that one does not learn from experience but rather tolerates having to think about its emotional force. Bion offers a second way to define experience, now as an emotional experience difficult to know. He is not so far away from James's view of the difficulty of knowing the other's mind. And he is not far away from Arendt's claim that we take responsibility for a world we live in. For Bion, knowing is an approximation, representations are not the thing-in-itself, and at some level the learning itself is unrepresentable. This is part of what is hated, I think, the hatred of frustration made from the experience of trying to represent what cannot be represented but only felt. Here is how Bion (1994b) presents the quandary: "If the learner is intolerant of the essential frustration of learning he indulges phantasies of omniscience and a belief in a state where things are known. Knowing something consists in "having" some "piece of" knowledge and not . . . 'knowing' in the sense of 'getting to know something'" (65). Our capacity to create value within emotional experience allows for new ideas and the experience of getting to know something new. No value is an attack on one's thinking; thinking is a way to render as valuable one's emotional experience. Being responsible for one's emotional experience opens an existential dimension, what Derrida (1994) called justice, or "hospitality without reservation" (65).

AN UNCANNY POSTMODERNITY

I have described teacher education as a conditioned field, in that all that it meets becomes a condition of its development. Because the field attempts to influence development, it is subject to hatred, its own and that of others. The childhood of education is a significant condition of our work, which means the field is subject to rejection, to schizoid processes, and to the hatred of development. I have suggested that how we conceptualize development will affect not only the ways in which we think about others and our knowledge but also how we feel about our own teacher education. And along with

Arendt, James, and Bion, I have suggested that the time of education is always out of joint. Briefly, I want to turn to the problem of the university itself as affected by what Arendt (1993b) called "the crisis of education."

The particular crisis universities face is the decline of enlightenment as a metaphor for education. In the last chapter, the decline was presented through Badiou's (2005) collapse of the pedagogic theme. From Arendt's view, our metanarratives have worn out. The general crisis is that the status of education and teaching has declined. Here uneven development takes on an institutional force. As a field of thought and practice, and as a site of knowledge production, institutions of education are affected by what Lyotard (1987) called "the postmodern condition." He was describing the state of knowledge use in postindustrial societies, and argued that the idea of knowledge as capable of training minds and as bringing up of culture (*bildung*) is now obsolete: knowledge itself changes so fast that its old use of changing minds is exhausted. As for the mind, it has been reduced to the function of processing data, and as the human extension of the information highway. We travel this highway as both consumers and producers, perhaps feeling knowledge as now something to display, access, and dispose of as quickly and as easily as possible. Yet the avalanche of information that both overgratifies and understimulates our postmodern soft pedagogy may leave us emptier than ever. Our postmodern condition has only quickened the way knowledge wears out. Knowledge is prepackaged, predigested, and disposable and it returns recycled as nostalgia. With this instrumentalism comes a new definition of the high-speed student, worried about falling behind. Learners must rush, become adept, flexible, and able to judge instant knowledge in terms of its use value, its applicability to real life concerns, and its prestige. It is too much to ask. But this means that skills supplant ideas, technique is confused with authority and responsibility, and know-how short-circuits the existential question of indeterminacy and incompleteness.

The expansion of multinational and now global corporations into every corner of our lives has terrific force in reshaping the university. Students, too, are consumers; they judge the competency of their education rather than their own efforts. They are potential litigators, clients with flimsy contracts. Teachers deliver a curriculum with no destiny. Excellence awards proliferate and are used to market the university, which must compete with other universities. Yet the pervasiveness of excellence awards has not always been the case, as Bill Readings (1996) remarked in his study of the university when he noted how excellent adventures have supplanted enlightenment narratives. The postmodern worker places new demands on the university—she is both consumer and unsatisfied customer. Readings's (1996) critique suggests the university is best described not as postmodern but as posthistorical. He means the university has lived beyond its founding values of "historical development, affirmation, and inculcation of national culture" (6). That is, the university performs the collapse of its pedagogic theme. Here is the new sense of where education wears out. The critical function of university education—to expand minds, to be critical of knowledge, to create personal and social insight—is obsolete. There is nothing to take responsibility for. In Readings's view, the significant quandary is how will we think of the social bond, community, recognition, responsibility, and difference if knowledge itself cannot put into place ethicality and if consumerism designs experience as excellent.

Our postmodern university complicates the childhood of teacher education and our work of taking responsibility for the world we have made. Indeed, we may ask, in the posthistorical university, has childhood itself become obsolete? What will the strange duration of childhood fixate on if experience is so fleeting and if knowledge itself becomes obsolete faster than it can be learned? What happens if our unconscious equation of development with loss is acted out by our technology? What then becomes of retroactive time, of uneven development? How will the slippery surface animate the depth of our soul? Is it now the case as Gertrude Stein once said, "There is no there, there"? Are we urged to enjoy such emptiness?

I want to propose that despite its shiny surface, the posthistorical university animates the depths of our dependency; we are even more dependent on the human condition than what we have previously understood. If we now understand that even our metanarratives wear out, their replacement with a thousand tiny relative narratives is just as fatiguing. And if we are no longer dependent on metanarratives, we are subject to how quickly they slip away and to the mental pain of trying to think. Before our eyes, we see the world wear out. This loss may provoke us to defend nostalgia, causing us to turn our backs on the crisis of education by fixating on what we imagine as a time before, when everything about experience was certain, when experience itself idealized its own structure of belief, and when emotional life was inadmissible to theory. This imaginary loss renders our education melancholic, filled with complaint that is then evacuated into the other who fails. Or, we might risk the emotional pain of thinking and symbolize education without the idealization of experience, itself a defense against the loss of experience. We might begin to ponder the problem that the experience we have and the having of experience has always been our crisis of education. We may come to think of what it means for education to lose its ideals, including the ideal of experience. Then, we may consider uncertainty as another term for what Arendt (1958) called the human condition, a relation that calls for us to think. In her own way, Arendt wrote:

> Men are conditioned because everything they come in contact with turns immediately into a condition of their existence. . . . The objectivity of the world—its object-or thing-character—and the human condition supplement each other; because human existence is conditioned existence, it would be impossible without things, and things would be a heap of unrelated articles, a non-world, if they were not the conditions of human existence. (9)

Our work, after all, like the world where we live, is always out of joint. And there are new problems experience cannot solve. Now, we have the absurd postmodern condition of sending our student teachers back to the nineteenth-century school where they encounter the twenty-first-century child. It is a condition that can feel like a "heap of unrelated things" even if such things are handmade.

The other problem for education is that there is no such thing as preparation for education and that learning to teach for the act of teaching and learning is an interminable problem of interpreting the frustration of incomplete experience. If teacher education is to matter to teachers, to the university, and to those who learn the work of teaching, our responsibility is to its conditions: learning to live in this time that is out of joint, in discontinuous time, and in the disjuncture of self/other relations. This means taking responsibility for the discomforting fact of our dependency on the unknown. Development is uneven because we are born too soon and become responsible for a world we have not made. If we have the strange work of trying to understand the minds of others and still keep our own mind, if we have the work of welcoming what cannot be understood and the responsibility for a hospitality without reserve, if we confront a world that is wearing out, and if we must work from all this ignorance, teacher education may begin. It will be a teacher education as an unfinished project, more fragile than we ever imagined, and now lost and found at the point where our fact of dependency develops within the promise of responsibility.

CHAPTER THREE

READING

———————

Dear Professor Britzman,
Thank you for assigning Never Let You Go.
       —Your student, K.

It is difficult to describe Ishiguro's (2005) novel, *Never Let Me Go*, without the uncanny experience of feeling oneself reading: something in these pages cannot be read. Does one encounter illegible experience or the anxiety of meeting it? Steiner (1980) relates unsettling reading events to an ontological difficulty, a disturbance in subterranean being, where, he argues, a contract is being broken: "*Ontological* difficulties confront us with blank questions about the nature of human speech, about the status of significance, about the construct which we have" (41). We become again slow readers, caught between our anticipations for what we hope to find and the consequences of the signifier that take us elsewhere. We lose our place. It can feel as if the book is reading us, turning our pages. When we read ourselves into this ontological difficulty, all that we bring to the literary experience cannot repair what breaks there. But why must our constructs fail? Does language itself betray the promise of communication?

The simplicity of the novel's plot lends anguish to reading's despair. Our narrator, Kathy H, is thirty-one years old. She is a clone looking back on a past that has no origin even as she speaks fondly of being sent to school.

Retroactive time collapses from memory's weight; she is never sure if the events she recalls match any meaning, then or now. Her story is affected. Everything feels mismatched and unclear. Early events register, leaving vague after-impressions. Later, accidental occurrences lift into terrible significance what is felt before it can be known. Meaning is deferred and her theories cannot help that. Her memories as fragments of life are addressed to us readers, and she always asks, "Do you know what I mean?" But we cannot know what she means, for her meanings will be too terrible to identify with and all we can do is stumble along with her through what feels like fields of disavowal. Kathy H has friends who are just like her and readers follow estranging development from their childhood spent in a boarding school to their terrible predestination. What will happen is this: after their education, the students' vital body parts—organ by organ—will be surgically removed and then transplanted into a human whose own body is threatened by its wear. In her anonymity she will replenish these "normals," as she calls them, service them until, as the normals will say, she "completes." Ironically, it is her education that will help her comply with this unreadable act.

Keep in mind that Kathy H and her cohorts are not machines. Nor do they fit in the strange category of technical innovation that Turkle (2006) calls "relational artifacts" (36), mechanical toys and robots created to service our affective functions. The difference is that while relational artifacts demand human care and are programmed to empathize and thus animate our human desire for recognition and attachment, these "students," as Ishiguro names them, are real and invoke horror because they can never be separated from their function and our cruelty. Unlike relational artifacts, where we care for these objects as if they are real and as if they can know our desires, Ishiguro takes away this "as if" quality and readers will feel a symbolic collapse. Literal creepiness leaves readers to question both the content of their own insides and the designs of the external world. What do we make of the humans who need to educate their spare parts? The novel's title can be read as ironic, in the way Lear (2003) describes its entanglements: "the speaker insists on holding onto what the words really do mean" (68). If irony never lets words go, what do we make of negation? What can *never* actually mean?

It is not only that Ishiguro's novel performs its own resistance to being read, itself a version of never letting go. And it is not just that Ishiguro presents readers with a peculiar ontological difficulty in the form of a negation novel narrated by a replicate-being, whose fate as a copy is to copy and replace a human part. While both dynamics in and of themselves—the uncanny, inquisitive creatures and the fate of their illegible design—present ontological difficulties, the anxiety of reading these part object creatures belongs to readers. My psychoanalytic reading explores this discord between the signifier and the signified, seeing such conflict as emblematic of any reading. I analyze the slow events of reading to illustrate two irresolvable conflicts animated and transferred onto the scene of reading: one belongs to an encounter with what is illegible yet impresses psychical reality, while the other concerns putting these impressions into language to speak and write about what is ambiguous and unknown in external reality. Ontic difficulties, though experienced from within, are constitutive of being with others; there is no ontology without the other. Even when we read external reality we cannot help drawing upon what is unresolved in our own reading archive—what we wish to see or never want to see again—yet, in so doing, the labor of reading reality follows the lines created by the transference. We hope the other receives our difficult communication. But our reading also returns to the reader to decipher. Reading, after all, animates the internal world of object relations and so provokes what Meltzer and Williams (1988) describe as "aesthetic conflict," an encounter with the enigmatic, unknown quality of the outside world tied both to our hope for finding beauty and our work of having to symbolize this search for life. Aesthetic conflicts remind us of our misreading: the ways we read regardless of what is presented, the way we read with desire and anxiety.

Where reading complicates and what confuses reading—where ontological difficulty becomes itself—is with the uncanny problem Ishiguro presents: readers are given a phantasy about our phantasy, a *mise-en-abîme*. The novel may be read as commentary on this dream within a dream, a story of origin and the carnival of the internal world of object relations that can overhear and then tries to read the society that invents them. The external world is known through these feeling-creatures so readers have the double work of identifying with characters they will also need to destroy and questioning what can be known at all since the untimely setting is a post-Darwinian society located in quaint villages in late twentieth-century England. This chronology, too, is without origin; it is administered through disequilibrium of language and education, guarded by impersonal science, populated by part objects, and made quite mad by a wish for no death and no birth.

The novel begins with a broken contract, a terrific collapse of the pedagogical theme. The resources we require for relationality, responsibility, and reparation of our object relations are, so to say, dangerous, secretive, paranoid, and persecutory. One aesthetic conflict resides in the problem of our being with language: how it is that we say one thing and mean something else, how it is that language deceives and compels our desire, how the other's overhearing cannot be controlled. Language can become euphemistic and consequently no longer addressed to anyone. Language can act out its own obscurantism to secure feigned knowledge. The other aesthetic conflict is inextricable, being tied to being with others. Repeatedly, the creatures in this novel wonder what they actually understand about their world when they are both told and not told about their fate. Left to their own theories, they carry out strange reality tests that lead them nowhere. It is not so much that knowledge is useless; its use is to destroy thinking.

Against these terrible odds, characters and readers persist in making meaning from the fog of language and its education: infantile theories proliferate and no one wants to let them go. Why this desire becomes animated is tied to that intimate conflict that constitutes psychical reality, what Klein (1930) simply called "unreal reality" (221). Here, then, are a few novel questions: suppose each of us could copy ourselves and that our affects are the copy. More difficult, suppose these copies are emissaries of our object relations, phantasies sent out into the world to do our own biddings. What can we make of our psychical constructions—our affects and desires—who then return to read us? Would we need to destroy them?

SLOW READINGS

Psychoanalytic readings are often accused of reading too much into our reading events, of taking poetic license, of presenting absence, and of treating the mind as if it is wanting and waiting to be read. Their readings, we may feel, are intrusive, hard to swallow, difficult to keep down. Anxiety irrupts where meaning is stretched to its further outpost, when the unconscious itself is approached as a stranger, as a meaning-making thing that obeys no laws. We refuse to be read by it, yet it still reads us. Psychoanalysis presents us with these reading problems, with the request that we become slow readers, but of another ilk than when we first learned to read in school. Then, the dilemma of slow readers is that they never let the word go because they will garble it, mistake it for something else, or worry about the direction the next word may take them. They stall precisely at the point where predictions are needed and worry that the predictions they make are wild guesses, off the mark. Their theory of reading—what they think should happen—may be too idealized, too loyal to the original text. Reading then becomes instrumental, a procedure for copying the text. Yet reading is not a matter of being able to decode conventional signs because meaning cannot fall into place with correct pronunciation. The problem with this sticky theory is that slow readers mistake competency for literal compliance. There is no wordplay between the signifier and the signified. Psychoanalytic accounts wonder about these fixations and insist that reading is the means for and function of our signifying interior world.

Felman (2003), for example, in her study of madness and literature, has named this force "the literary thing . . . the original, originative drive that makes us read" (5). We cannot stop reading the literary thing; it can never let us go. Jacobus's (1999) study on "the scene of reading" leads her to question the work of reading. She likens reading to transference, perhaps recalling Freud's (1912) view of the transference as both an inquiry addressed to the other and the resistance to the meaning one cannot anticipate, that is, the unexpected reply. Jacobus explores the resistance to reading when she raised the Kleinian problem of inhibition, the painful experience of holding oneself back from reading, of, say, not being able to let go of the original object and allow interpretation to enliven and even change its meaning. Sedgwick (1997) will see in reading inhibitions the Kleinian paranoid-schizoid position, but also, in its oscillation, a potential she terms "reparative practices" (8).

Klein understood intellectual inhibition as a defense against an inaugural anxiety that reading provokes: in wanting both to know and not know one's origins, the child becomes agitated and feels barred from possessing the contents of the mother's body. The preoccupation is with what cannot be seen and what cannot be known, our first aesthetic conflict. Klein (1932) posits the drive to know as flowering from archaic sadism, itself a developmental requirement. In Klein's formulation there is a terrible prolepsis: knowing is first equated with destroying the object, then worrying if the object will retaliate, then wondering about one's own destructive capacities. Doubt, guilt, and grief, or depressive anxiety, accompany the desire for gratitude and reparation. The object of knowledge only gradually emerges from this thicket of projections and identifications. Reading leans on this archaic constellation of anxiety, for we actually need to project into the text, tear it apart before it retaliates, and then put it back together again through our "reparative" reading, which is why the interpretation of this transference matters. Klein (1932) insisted on the importance of others to contain this developmental rage: "the mother has to prove again and again by her presence that she is not the 'bad', attacking mother. The child requires a real object to combat its fear of its terrifying introjected objects and of its super-ego. Furthermore, the presence of the mother is used as evidence she is not dead" (179). It is the mother's love that enlivens, urging the child to risk, through symbolization, a new relation with itself and its first object. This power of love will be the significant resource for the ego to find and encounter a reality beyond phantasy and to reencounter phantasy's reading purpose.

Klein's (1931) analysis of a boy who could not distinguish a series of words (poulet, chicken; poisson, fish; glace, ice), or understand why these particular words came to represent dead, gray, crawly things for him, mentions James Strachey's work on reading:

> J. Strachey (1930) has shown that reading has the unconscious significance of taking knowledge out of the mother's body, and that fear of robbing her is an important factor for inhibitions in reading. I should like to add that it is essential for a favourable development of the desire for knowledge that the mother's body should be felt to be well and unharmed. It represents in the unconscious the treasure-house of everything desirable which can only be got from there; therefore if it is not destroyed, not so much in danger and therefore not so dangerous itself, the wish to take food for the mind from it can be more easily carried out. (241)

Yet there is nothing easy in Klein's view of embodiment since it begins in disembodiment and this anxiety constitutes both the dilemma and the potential life, since the ontological difficulty is a radical relation. There is no being without being with the other.

Reading feels as if it begins with taking in, introjecting the text/body and projecting meanings back into it. In the logic of emotions, introjection is our turn to the act of copying the object, only to project it back into the world, now accompanied by our own difference. These psychological preludes threaten to destroy the good object by turning it into the bad, vengeful one, which then, in turn, threatens to destroy both the copy and the original. There is paranoia and splitting—the paranoid schizoid position—that both animates and creates introjection and projection and in the logic of phantasy, there is no distinction between introjection and projection. Both bring dangers. Yet this act founds the object relation because introjection and projection are the procedures for identification, itself the basis for creating and destroying libidinal social bonds. Jacobus's (1999) use of both Klein and Strachey leads her to consider reading as mental digestion. She must also suppose something negative: indigestion, diarrhea, eating one's words, and vomiting them out. Reading is likened to either a good feed or a forced one. One of the satisfactions of a good read is that we may refind, in the mind, objects that have been lost to the world. Forced readings render this search futile, but also return us to the oral stage.

We can expand Jacobus's discussion to include the idea that reading recapitulates development or even that it copies development. And this puts a strain on reading, turning reading troubles into emotional distress. Klein will take a further leap into this phantasy: if reading copies development, it is because in psychical life there is no originary moment, only the body of the other that feeds and contains the neonate. From this act of taking in, which, in some sense is taking in what has already been expelled—what Klein calls projective identification—the object relations needed to evolve these precocious resources into symbolization, interpretation, and creativity are created. From object relations, which have no origin, one may find the difference between the symbol and the thing, or the difference between the signifier and the signified, and then the difference between the self and the other. Paradoxically, for this relationship to be recognized there must be a separation. The object must be let go to permit the self and the other their reading lives. At the heart of creating internal and external reality, however, separation is equated with loss and a terrible fear of destroying reality. The ontological difficulty is that if this fear is also needed, lest we become monstrous, it is also where a contract is being broken.

Only some of these developmental processes will occur for Ishiguro's "students." Or, if they occur, they reverse their order. Indeed, just as we feared, there only are bad attacking others and no evidence of a mother's life. Our ontological difficulty with Ishiguro's novel begins when we wonder if these students represent emissaries from the internal world even as they have their own internal world. Yet how can there be an internal world without introjecting the first object, the mother's breast? These replica students were never born, but, inexplicably, they desire, they love, they want recognition. Here is where my own reading broke down, where I became, again, a slow reader, searching for the literal origin of meaning and not being able to let go.

How can this novel be read? Shall we see the novel as an allegory for interiority? Or is it a parable of childrearing and so a comedy of error made from forbidden parental Oedipal wishes? What if the novel is the educator's phantasy: that teachers, in the ways in which they prepare students, do have a hand in murdering them? Is it a phantasy that students have: that the teachers and anyone else really want to eat them because they cannot be original? Is this our worry about copying and being copied? Is it a story of not seeing what is in front of one's eyes? Could this novel be what Jacobus (2005), in her discussion of the poetics of Kleinian play and the work of Susan Isaacs, identifies as an "acting out of metaphor" (96)? Does language have agency? What can it mean for the metaphor to turn against its object, to take on a life of its own, and to wreak havoc? Is this science fiction or fairy tale? How can a copy have real feelings if there is no original object, if there is no mother? What makes these copies so real that their theory of love allows them to imagine, against all odds, a refinding of the lost object? These student creatures present what Klein (1957) called "memories in feelings" (180). Indeed, in the last pages of the novel, our narrator, Kathy H, feels that no one can take her memories away, even if she herself is disposable. Kathy H must die from a phantasy of social eugenics that has replaced introjection and projection with the surgical procedures of transplantation. There is only possessing the other and never letting go. In this phantasy world, ontological difficulties belong to no one. The phantasy is that one cannot read because the text is set. The phantasy is that we must overread, read into our own insides.

COPYCATS

Our reading methods, or the theories we use to protect and project our own intelligibility, may initially foreclose this reading trauma, what Arendt (1993a), in her discussion of Kantian action and history, called a confrontation with "melancholy haphazardness" (85). One effect of melancholy is also a defense against it: we wish for a doppelgänger. Dreams permit us to double ourselves, to have a second-chance self. Each night we may project our mistakes and wishes into the body of someone just like us. And every night we may take our novel time to play all of the roles, becoming again slow readers. The child's imaginary twin performs this service as well, along with our stories of neonates being given to the wrong family. Anxiety's delegates give reasons, intentions, wishes, and purposes to our bad objects.

Ishiguro narrates the doppelgänger's enigma: here is a society that engineers its own greedy immortality, a social state that cannot lose the object, cannot wear out and so will neither die nor recognize love. We are presented with the paranoid schizoid position: the mother's body cannot be robbed because it is already full of stolen goods. And as for the reader's identification, we may have to ask what we are analyzing when we analyze the novel, when we analyze our relation to this particular phantasy that invites something of our own obsession, anxiety, and paranoia, our misreading. For what we have is a copy reading our worst phantasies of destruction: mother's body is dead because she feeds upon her children. And this body/novel both fascinates and disgusts. We encounter, then, a terrible love story, in which the Kleinian contract of love as reparation, as atonement for the destruction and as gratitude toward the other, is being broken.

Kathy H carries the donors' memories but also their mysteries, for these replicas have real feelings and so they, too, search for the meaning of life, anxiously gathering discarded clues, patching together hearsay and hope and proposing, from this refuge, a preposterous theory: even if the contract is broken, there may be a hidden loophole of escape. Their questions are the inverse of the Kleinian child, for essentially Kathy H and her friends will end up as the inside of the mother's body: they provide her treasures and so their curiosity, their drive to know, cannot affect the other. Here is the literary thing in overdrive. Their attempts at symbolization cannot reach the heights of tragedy or the Kierkegaardian sense of despair, of not wanting to be who one is; compliance literally keeps them together until, that is, it is time for them to be torn apart.

On the last pages of the novel, Kathy H is mourning for her lover, Tommy. They have let each other go because Tommy is about to expire. She is standing on a flat field, surveying all the rubbish, and then has "a fantasy thing" (263) that went no further:

> I was thinking about the rubbish, the flapping plastic in the branches . . . and I half closed my eyes and imagined this was the spot where everything I'd ever lost since my childhood had washed up. . . . The fantasy never got beyond that—I didn't let it—and though the tears rolled down my face, I wasn't sobbing or out of control. I just waited a bit, then turned back to the car, to drive off to wherever it was I was supposed to be. (263)

But the "fantasy thing" is not really over. After all, there is still the drive.

Kathy H, along with her peers, has spent her childhood in a school called Hailsham. Its name means what it says: the children, with no parents, are greeted by a sham that they can't quite figure but that manages to hail them. Their teacher-guardians seem to give them an education, but no assignment has any purpose. The rules of the school are secretive, leaving the students alone to wildly interpret their guardian's utterances. In this pretend school the students are urged to be creative and to make art, which is collected by Madame. Kathy H has a few unexpected run-ins with Madame: she hopes Madame can understand her, but their interactions leave both disturbed. Ruth, one of Kathy's strange friends, believes Madame is afraid of the students. In one scene, six of the eight-year-old girls decide to "swarm" Madame. They want her reaction. They wanted to scare her, pretending they were in a dream. But the girls had an incomplete plan:

> And it wasn't even as though Madame did anything other than what we predicted she'd do: she just froze and waited for us to pass by. She didn't shriek, or even let out a gasp. But we were all so keenly tuned in to picking up her response, and that's probably why it had such an effect on us. . . . And I can

> still see it now, the shudder she seemed to be suppressing, the real dread that
> one of us would accidentally brush against her. . . . Ruth was right: Madame
> *was* afraid of us. But she was afraid of us in the same way someone might be
> afraid of spiders. We hadn't been ready for that. It never occurred to us to
> wonder how *we* would feel, being seen like that, being the spiders. (32)

There is no way to prepare for one's strangeness and Kathy H takes a moment
to teach us readers about our universal selves: "I'm sure somewhere in your
childhood, you too had an experience like ours that day; similar if not in the
actual details, then inside, in the feelings" (33).

MISUNDERSTANDING

The problem of reading also belongs to the realm of thought and desire, what
Arendt (1958) considered as narrative. The labor of thought questions how
one reconciles reality with truth, separates the meaningful from the meaningless, and judges the consequences of action when acting cannot guarantee
thought and may even destroy it. Desire gives the gift of the question and thus
places us in the world with others. But for Arendt (1993a), a terrible blind spot
or ignorance propels human action:

> Human action, like all strictly political phenomena, is bound up with
> human plurality, which is one of the fundamental conditions of human life
> insofar as it rests on the fact of natality, through which the human world
> is constantly invaded by strangers, newcomers whose actions and reactions
> cannot be foreseen by those who are already there and are going to leave in
> a short while. (61)

The replenishing of life, in Arendt's view, repeats its own fragility: because
the future cannot be known, welcoming the stranger and feeling invaded go
hand in hand. Natality with its promise, and life with its constraints, all turn
on relations of existence and generations and so, on life and death. Except in
the novel, those already here will not leave: they will not let go, they hate the
stranger, and there is no plurality. Thought is banal and evil. Concerned as
she is with the question of the political, itself a reflection of the limitations of
human action, Arendt (1993a), in her epilogue to her essay on history, links
desire without the second chance of thought to the paranoid-schizoid totalitarian society:

> In my studies of totalitarianism I tried to show that the totalitarian phe-
> nomenon, with its striking anti-utilitarian traits and its strange disregard
> for factuality, is based in the last analysis on the conviction that everything

is possible—not just permitted, morally or otherwise . . . that action can
be based on any hypothesis and that, in the course of consistently guided
action, particular hypothesis will become true, will become actual, factual
reality. The assumption which underlies consistent action can be as mad as
it pleases. (87)

The totalitarian society can be as mad as it pleases because everything is possible, including control of reality and life. But this means something terrible:
nothing can be human, because even possibility wears itself down. That other
totalitarian society, the one the psychoanalysts euphemistically term omnipotence, also refuses to read into its desire to be the law.

Arendt's (1958) discussion of the human condition describes natality as
fragile, new, and ushering in promise. She is careful to separate the human
condition, or what is public, from human nature, which she considers private.
This distinction is not easily maintained, for, without the private, there would
be no public and a public without the private is no public at all. Her stress,
however, is on the condition: "men are conditioned beings because everything they come in contact with turns immediately into a condition of their
existence" (9). But here we meet another problem because human nature,
whatever that can mean, is also our condition. Even as Arendt insists on places
where one can narrate hope for new beginnings, something within human
nature is blind to its conditions. She writes: "The miracle that saves the world,
the realm of human affairs, from its normal, "natural" ruin is ultimately the
fact of natality, in which the faculty of action is ontologically rooted. It is, in
other words, the birth of new men and the new beginning, the action they
are capable of by virtue of being born" (247). The haphazard melancholia,
for both Ishiguro and Arendt, is that action can be an act of disavowal and a
hatred of life, a severing of a responsibility yet to become. The problem is that
action cannot know its own duration or consequences. We may be capable of
actions, but our actions can render us incapable as well.

What saves us from ourselves, according to Arendt, is that others are
born. This is a curious insistence, for it suggests that our second chance does
not belong to us. Ishiguro's novel severs this second chance by supposing the
psychoanalytic mythology of the Oedipal conflict in reverse: rather than the
child wanting to have one parent and kill the other one, it is the parents who
will kill the child and refuse the law of mortality and incest. There is no law.
Language becomes truncated, made euphemistic: there are replicas, the normals, they and us, models, carers, donors, and no name-of-the-father. With
the veil of deception that is language, the desire for recognition, a relation
that also saves the world, or, at least, offers a lifeline between those yet to

become and those already here, unravels. And when there is no recognition, as Ricoeur (2005) has shown, there is no gratitude for being recognized. Recognition, for Ricoeur, is not the work of identification and categorization, but the work of gratitude: the one who gives recognition takes responsibility and gives reparation, the one who receives recognition gives gratitude. Recognition institutes the social bond, but is itself organized by misrecognition: "The test of misunderstanding . . . shakes our confidence in the capacity of things and persons to make themselves recognized. An acceptance of a kind of companionship with misunderstanding, which goes with the ambiguities of an incomplete, open-ended life world, has to replace the fear of error" (256–257).

THEORIES

Our student clones attempt to make into a companion their feelings of being misunderstood. While they tried to express themselves by making art, no one knew why they were required to hand their art over. From reading novels and from her teachers' lectures, Kathy H patches together the romantic dream that art is an expression of the artist's soul. If art holds the secret of the artist's soul, if art somehow can telegraph the secret yearnings of the artist—that the artist loves, lives, desires, possesses depth, and can symbolize all of this—she reasoned, her wish for recognition must also reflect her humanity. And, in one way, having their art collected by Madame and placed in The Gallery could confirm her desire, except the students do not know if such a place even exists. Against all odds, they make their theories and want to test them. One theory carries the students through adolescence and into their adulthood. It is, so to say, a faint hope clause because the students both know and do not know their fate; they have been told and not told; they believe and do not believe. Their theory is tied to the shadowy figure of Madame who quickly enters the school and leaves with their art. She is stealing their treasures.

The teachers tell the students they are special. It is a designation that dissolves every meaning into fog. There are ghastly truths to learn, but, before that, the students are captured by their theories and myths: lost and murdered children, limbs that suddenly drop off of bodies, and even phantasies of having a normal life, like those they find in the magazines. Everything is unfathomable, secrets are being kept, hints cannot be read, and contracts are being broken. They have learned to become slow readers sorting through the enigmatic signifier. And they find reasons everywhere, but to no purpose. If the school itself turned the students into detectives, they reasoned, and if whispering was the preferred mode of exchange, then all meanings would have to be arranged and rearranged on the sly, sutured quickly while no one was looking. Tommy's theory comes after Miss Lucy, a teacher, tells him not to imagine his future. Before Miss Lucy was fired, she tells her charges: "The problem, as I see it, is you've been told and not told . . . and none of you understand. . . . Your lives are set out for you. You'll become adults, then before you're old, before you're even middle aged, you'll start to donate your vital organs. That's what each of you was created to do" (73). Yet the adolescents cannot understand what this means and, undoubtedly, no one can. The students are suddenly embarrassed, as if Miss Lucy had lost her mind. For the adolescents, what will happen could only be joked about, even if there were strange worries of the body becoming unzipped, or arms suddenly falling off. They made impossible remedies to avoid falling apart. And the teachers urged them to take care of their bodies, but without ever saying why.

DEFERRAL

Years later, Tommy, the boy with inexplicable temper tantrums who refused to be creative and make art as a child, recalled something Miss Emily once said: "Things like pictures, poetry, all that kind of stuff, she said, they revealed what you were inside, she said. They revealed your soul" (160). If the guardians looked to the art as evidence of the students' soul, the students reasoned, they would also be able to understand themselves if only they could have a look at their "models," or the "possibles," people the students hoped might be their parents. An odd reversal occurs, for the students believe their parents would hold the key to what might have been their future. The students combed through television characters, the magazine models, the pornography pictures, trying to understand why they felt as they did but also to learn new feelings. Kathy H manically flips through pornography, hoping to see a parent there. Perhaps seeing a porn star would explain her inexplicable desire to have meaningless sex. When, after graduating from Hailsham, they are sent to a waiting camp for "training," where nothing actually happened, the students would sneak into town, looking for models they thought would be the key to their own insides. But how old would the models be? Would they be parents or babies? Kathy H explains:

> Since each of us was copied at some point from a normal person, there must be, for each of us, someone out there, a model getting on with his or her life. . . . One big idea behind finding your model was that when you did, you'd glimpse your future. . . . We . . . believed that when you saw the

person you were copied from, you'd get some insight into who you were deep down, and maybe too, you'd see something of what your life held in store. (127)

This was the dream future, where reason merges desire with certainty. It is also the adolescent belief, a fixation described by Kristeva (2007): "The adolescent is not a researcher in a laboratory, he's a believer. We are all adolescents when we are enthralled by the absolute" (717). And, what could be more absolute than meeting your copy?

Late in the novel, the students have grown up to live their life as donations. Hailsham has closed. The school had an impossible mission: to educate organs under the guise of humane treatment for the students. The founders wanted to give these creatures a childhood and perhaps a memory of that. Certainly Kathy H learned this affected lesson, for she is narrating her story and her own ending. Now in their thirties and finally consummating their long love affair, Kathy H and Tommy recall the art that Madame collected, their expressions that revealed their insides, their souls. Years before, they heard vague rumors that Madame grants a year's deferral for surgery if the couple can prove they are really in love. They feel they are not asking for much, only one year's grace. The aging students find Madame and Miss Emily to ask for their deferral, only to learn that no such possibility ever existed. The deferral was only a rumor, a runaway desire. But why take the art away, and why have Hailsham? asks Kathy H. "Miss Emily said, 'Yes, why Hailsham at all . . . We took away your art because we thought it would reveal your souls. Or, to put it more finely, we did it to *prove you had souls at all.*' Kathy H replies, 'Why did you have to prove a thing like that, Miss Emily? Did someone think we didn't have souls?'" (237–238). And Miss Emily then knew that her educational experiment worked: the students could be "taken aback." She missed, however, how these students returned the improbability of her surprising reading. What she could not know is their negation: the reply, "I do not understand." What the students could not know as well is that they already had their deferral called childhood and they made that from their inexplicable wish to know their own insides.

In the allegory that is reading, our copies cannot know themselves as copies, nor do our phantasies know their own negations. Psychoanalytic reading teaches us a lesson we already know, that we cannot let go of affected life— we are always reading between the lines, wagering meaning and deferring it. Here is where we find that our constructs fail. Illegible experience turns us into slow readers, returning us to a time before language when oral and anal phases reign supreme, where introjecting the world and projecting it back into the world of others mark and read ontological difficulty. If Ishiguro's novel presents us with our phantasies of being born without parents, of our worries that we may have to donate our insides, of having to go to school without knowing why, of always having to fail our reading comprehension tests, of having sexuality without reason, and of the wishing for immortality with our little hope for a deferral—indeed, of never having to let go—he also reminds us that these phantasies may take on a life of their own, and in some sense may need to in order for us to read at all. In the strangest of ways, Ishiguro writes of reading's development and returns us to our private never-never-land. In this regard, what makes us all special students is that the anxiety of reading belongs to us; that when we read, we really do rob someone's insides, we really do read into things. The act of being a slow reader performs these ontological difficulties, something needed for symbolization and art as well. While experienced from within, ontological difficulties, what Klein (1930) simply called "unreal reality," (221) and reading into this involve a work of belonging to others and a second chance.

CHAPTER FOUR

PSYCHOLOGY

What was life? No one knew. It was aware of itself the moment it became life, that much was certain—and yet it did not know what it was. . . . Consciousness of self was an inherent function of matter once it was organized as life, and if that function was enhanced it turned against the organism that bore it, strove to fathom and explain the very phenomenon that produced it, a hope-filled and hopeless striving of life to comprehend itself, as if nature were rummaging to find itself in itself—ultimately to no avail, since nature cannot be reduced to comprehension, nor in the end can life listen to itself.

—Thomas Mann, *The Magic Mountain*

TELOS

Not much is certain about representing our affected psychology, about turning affect into language, and about learning from within this uncertainty. If we then turn to the field of psychology for answers as to what we are about, we may attribute our anxiety to its content, weighted by the burden of explaining human development and its problems of mind, motivation, behavior, and character. Its hearing may burn our ears. Psychology, after all, is talking about us. And if we find in its language our paranoia, our obsessionality, our perversions, and our neurosis, it is only because we are already psychological beings. In Piera Aulagnier's (2001) view, it takes a psychology to make a psychology

61

and our sounding begins the moment our first other draws us into "the plea-sure of hearing, the desire to hear, [and] the demand for meaning" (57). This much is certain: as pleasure turns to demand for love and for meaning, we become subject to the symbolic, and to our own overhearing, mishearing, and refusing to listen. As soon as the erotic body vibrates with anticipation for the other, as soon as we become aware of ourselves, as soon as we become self-conscious and thus vulnerable to our thoughts about these thoughts, we both want and do not want what we find. And the questions that follow, an echo of our resounding desire, may also unnerve us.

But if it takes a psychology to make a psychology, the field called psychol-ogy eludes this transference neurosis and its own anthropomorphic nature. It is as if it writes with an invisible hand. When Foucault (2006) approached the field of psychology as apparatus, practice, and as object of knowledge/power/pleasure, he found its history of forgetting within the receding vantage of madness and how the human sciences passed over this with their insistence on a discourse of mental illness. He related this genealogy of knowledge to its three domains: power, ethics, and pleasure. Together they impress and call forth our fault lines with meanings of normality and pathology. As a mecha-nism and function of power, knowledge raised for Foucault the question of how and when the human became posited as a psychological being, subject to its own interiority and to those of others. As ethics, Foucault asked how the human becomes a problem for the impossible professions of medicine, edu-cation, and government. The pleasure domain, from whatever side, lends to these procedures of knowledge the erotic charge of mastery and identity tied to the desire to look, to examine, to auscultate, and to be seen, examined, and heard.

The metaphors of psychology register these conflicts: exchanging mad-ness with biology, bringing discourse to observation, and reconstituting evo-lution with ecology. One consequence of these great discursive knowledge shifts is that the more the human's vulnerability and limitation become tied to the progress of science, the more science becomes silent about its own affected history. Another consequence follows: this silent history speaks, now from the vantage of what it does not say but nonetheless acts out. In Foucault's (2006) view: "In the reconstruction of this experience of madness, a history of the conditions of possibility of psychology wrote itself as though of its own accord" (xxxiv). It is as if the field of psychology repeated our own Oedipal mythology of love and hate, wishing to give itself birth while still needing to kill its parents and have the baby. Even as psychology's new century turns from the language of psychical conflicts to those of cognitive deficits, it continues writing "its own accord," now with another discourse, one that Fodor (2007) ironically calls "panpsychism." Left to its own accord, consciousness is presented as an endless production of itself: as the cause, consequence, effect, and condition for its own mastery.

As the psychological field turns toward the biology of cognition, the mind is thought to emerge from and function with the gray matter of tiny neurons, themselves actions upon actions (Doidge 2007). Impulses are hiring, firing, and misfiring themselves, forming pathways of vast circuitry that somehow stimulate and inhibit bodily functions with links to desire. The idea is that the brain is plastic, endlessly creating itself, and capable of making up its own mind. Certainly others are needed for these affairs, yet the solipsism of the field's imagery of multiplying and dividing neurons lends to the brain, and to the field, a weird autonomy. Big questions must follow: why are circuits subject to breakdown? Who fixes them? Who comprehends what? But also, if the mind can be anything, why would it go to such great lengths to deceive it? These questions are foreclosed as the applications of neuroscience enter the field of education. We find ourselves subject to endless practices of cognitive improvement programs, repetitive memory tasks, motivational advice, and exercises to reorder the brain. Without much comment, the new catchwords are learning and unlearning, accomplished through the baby steps of positive thoughts supported by rewards. We are urged to enjoy our education.

And yet the capacity for consciousness to know its own procedures as it thinks and that education can have its way here—to say nothing of what it feels like and can mean to symbolize the history of our own insides, indeed, to wonder how this gray matter comes to matter at all—remains ineffable. We cannot know the meaning of life, nor can we even say why we have meaning at all. Not even neuroscience can touch the affective vulnerabilities of learning made from unanswerable questions and our pleasure and terror in having to ask them. We cannot give ourselves reasons for our reasons. Nor can we leave the language of psychology to account for why psychology makes us nervous.

Second thoughts may bring us to the heart of the matter: the psychological subject must take itself as its own object of knowledge, moving deeper into its own psychology, but in that process incurs self-alienation through turning against the self. We can only objectify the self with something nonobjective: our projections. Through projecting into our own identifications, we also are gambling with a constitutive alienation for the hope of refinding our own lost cause and unity. This is the tragic condition of the bodily ego that Freud (1923, 26) described: a projection of its own surface that can then take itself as its own love object but also become the cause of its own derision. It is almost as if, in its very process of coming to know, the ego encounters the history of its own losses. And yet, without absence, there would be no reason to symbolize. Only humans struggle to fill this lack with becoming who they are. As Lacan saw it, all in the name of truth, humans are the only animals capable of self-deception, illusion, and disillusion. Humans are the only creatures who link and sever their authenticity for the other's desire (Lacan 1998b).

Psychoanalysis begins with this history of otherness: how need turns to want and then migrates into demand, how in this occurrence love and hate are never so far apart, and then how we come to want to give birth to ourselves only to find a discord in our own accord. These conflicts posit and divide the human and give us their remainder: psychical life. In this narrative, consciousness, as the exception rather than the rule of life, serves as a protective barrier against intolerable stimuli and the violence of the real. Its other is the unconscious, an unknowable force of antihistory made from desires without contradiction, negativity, or time. And psychoanalysis gives the function of biology away for this problem of having to symbolize. "We owe it to psychoanalysis," writes Aulagnier (2001), "to have shown that the need for the presence of an Other is in no way reducible to the vital functions that it must carry out" (72). Leaning on the other leaves us with our own inexplicable remainder: our psychical life.

Given its own conditions of possibility—that psychology must incorporate, defer, and repress that which is beyond it—neither the field called psychology nor we as psychological beings can comprehend with reason a crisis of subjectivity that the human must suffer in order to develop. That we are unnerved by any psychology is the return of this repressed. And one aspect of this crisis emerges from something that is not gray matter but feels like it, what Lacan (1998a) calls " the status of knowledge [that] raise[s] another question, namely how it is taught" (141). In this turn to education that is yet to come, Lacan was not suggesting a better teaching technique to make psychology digestible, for he saw instituted education itself as a defense against desire and urged us to think of something indigestible about our psychology. In placing the problem of knowledge into the question of how it is taught, Lacan returned us to the crisis of education from the vantage of a style of teaching and learning (Felman 1987).

Let us consider our discomforting psychology as it is linked to teaching and learning with the idea that there is an ontic crisis magnified when one tries to think of the mind and body as composed of gray matter, chemical procedures, networks of neurons firing and misfiring, or even when one encounters representations of the mind and its affects as radically relational and as unbound by consciousness and its projection of bodily boundaries, time, and space. From this problem we may slowly make our way to the idea that ontic crisis—the anticipating body that attempts to confront the real—is also a resource for hope and the condition for how Klein (1940) presented "the depressive position" (345), a change in the procedures of thought and feeling, conveyed through the poignancy and risks of love. Klein linked the adult's work of mourning losses to the development of a child's mind. She believed that learning emerged with the conflict between the hope for goodness and the anxiety of its loss. In this relationship, Klein's theory may be used to link learning with the wish to restore and repair one's inner and outer world.

While discussions of neuroscience play a role in the problems sketched, my aim is neither to argue with this science nor to idealize a time when the mind was not likened to plasticity, wireless networks, and automata functions. Yet knowing how something works does not give rise to a theory of learning. Nor is the specification of the mind's functions the same as experiencing our feelings through words. I will raise some special difficulties that affect us because the field of neuroscience is presented as having a capacity to reorder human behavior and reorganize, without much critical comment, our values and attitudes toward what can count as order and disorder, as error and pathology, and as progress and regression. If education is always affected by the question of how knowledge should be taught, received, and retained and in this way is always on the verge of suffering from its own memory disorder, the field of neuroscience now pressures it with what can count as hope and hopelessness, and education and malediction.

We don't really need the field of psychology to feel this vulnerability since we cannot help anthropomorphizing the mind and populating it with a strange combination of our own creaturely life and our dearly held and feared objects. Taking in and spitting out is the beginning of psychology (Aulagnier 2001). Try as we might to bend this beginning into relevancy or subject it to memory, however, it takes us to the limits of consciousness. There is no cure to prevent inner causality from its compelling libidinality and its adhesive expression through procedures of introjection, projection, identification, and transference. Nor can we understand with certainty the odd occurrence of needing to disavow reality and history without realizing why. And there is no answer our defenses can give us as to why the human feels the urge to dominate nature, no ultimate reason why affective life may be rendered as irrational and as something to overcome.

While there are a great many contexts one may call upon to understand this crisis of meaning and so of subjectivity, the field of education provides our transit point, specifically the classroom, since the ideas of general psychology and now cognitive science tend to be introduced, conveyed, and disseminated there. Lectures are still the technology of choice in university courses, yet rarely do we link this knowledge's dissemination to a constitutive conflict in subject/object relations. While students and teachers feel a great deal of anxiety over the uses and meaning of psychology as they anticipate how their own psychology is conveyed by them and received by the other, these affects take their force from the primal scene of our first education, where the other's knowledge addresses both our ignorance and desire, and where, through our lawless sense of being, our unconscious registers what neither party ever consciously intended. This unprecedented mismatch is repeated in teaching and learning, and, if all goes well, is a part of what is studied.

To understand the problems of representing psychology, I turn to the psychological lectures of Freud, Winnicott, and Adorno, each of whom links, with different emphasis, the crisis of subjectivity to problems in teaching and learning. The genre of lecture itself is instructive because the lecturer is making an attempt to communicate a style of teaching and learning without really knowing how the knowledge will be heard. Not knowing can be one of our most honest admissions in educational settings, unless, of course, the lecturer becomes nervous. In the case of the psychoanalysts, much psychoanalytic knowledge has been conveyed through the lecture, usually peppered with commentary on teaching style, resistance to learning, and objections to its theories. It is this seasoned knowledge that confers on these lectures their problems in symbolization. They all convey an antipedagogical flavor with the acknowledgment of learning's latency. These lectures turn on the question of affect, taking their residence within a paradox of human learning, first raised by Anna Freud and then heightened by Klein (Britzman 2003a). The problem is that there can be no learning or teaching without anxiety, yet anxiety, an anticipation and story of self/other relations, calls forth both phantasies of and desires for knowledge and defenses against its loss. But if anxiety signals that first urge to think, it is also the force in which thoughts lose their curiosity. Anxiety exchanges what does not yet exist in the name of what has already happened.

To glimpse what it feels like to think the psychology of our psychology, I then turn to two novels, which also have their own lectures. They reside in that other gray area, literary knowledge, what Felman (1987) theorizes as a knowledge that cannot be in charge of itself, yet charges its readers to think differently about how we experience our conflicts with mastery, progress, and difference. Thomas Mann's (2005) *Magic Mountain* and Richard Powers's (2006) *The Echo Maker* are novels of illness and education. They can be thought of as historical bookends to the question of teaching and learning psychology. They play in the ruins of the collapse of their pedagogical themes. Each novel presents a protagonist's crisis of development as coincident with world crisis and his thoughts on life and death. Their genre is the *Zeitroman*, novels critical of their own age; indeed, they represent a literary register of disillusionment with the promise of progress, education, and cure. These time novels are well equipped to service our own imagination, itself a peculiar disorder of the mind needed to interpret the erotic force of teaching and learning. Mann's novel opens the twentieth century as affected by its coincidental technologies of interiority: the X-ray machine, discovered in Germany 1895 and psychoanalysis, discovered around the same time in Vienna by Freud's hysterics and then through his own dream life. These shadowy inventions—a special introduction to our own otherness—open the body to questioning its mysterious interiority. Our young unformed hero, Hans Castorp, spends his time novel in a sanitarium where he learns from others how to be ill. Over the course of his long stay, Hans receives many lectures on psychology and education and gets lost in its thickets.

Powers's novel plunges readers into our twenty-first century. It, too, is affected with the technology of its time such as neuroscience, the Internet, the cell phone, the global economy and their contribution to the "post 911" mentality of paranoia, surveillance, information, and fear of falling. Our late-in-life hero, Gerald Weber, is a neurophysiologist in the midst of falling into his own nervous breakdown. He, too, learns from others how to be ill, but not before he ruins his own empire of neuroscience, originally dedicated to knowing and popularizing its cases. Despite his intentions, Weber could not help himself from being affected by the strange and estranging world of neurological disorders. And like his patients and students, Weber has difficulty with recognition. His disorder repeats what cannot be symbolized by the knowledge he holds; he only learns this while giving a lecture. I conclude with the ontic question of the crisis of meaning as a human condition needed for what Lear (2006) calls "radical hope." Here education as both cultural process and psychological experience may encounter new ways to question our recourse to mastery and the defenses against difference that follow. From this ruin the enigmatic qualities of our culture and mind do become needed resources, even if one cannot know where these resources lead.

LECTURES

Freud was the first lecturer on the problem of taking in and spitting out psychoanalysis. He already knew that psychology makes us nervous. Indeed, over the course of his career, he wrote many lectures on this topic and his (1933[1932]) *New Introductory Lectures on Psycho-analysis* began with a poignant admission:

> These new lectures, unlike the former ones, have never been delivered . . . a surgical operation had made speaking in public impossible for me. If, therefore, I once more take my place in the lecture room during the remarks that follow, it is only by an artifice of the imagination; it may help me not to forget to bear the reader in mind as I enter more deeply into my subject. (5)

But keeping the reader in mind meant having to argue with her and with his own doubts in assuming the depths of his speculations. Perhaps he was also speaking then to himself when he advised his readers to expect haziness, indeed, to accompany him through the bewildering haze of the mind. The request is difficult and Freud knew too well that, when it comes to the matter of psychology, readers only want to know what they already believe with the insistence on confirming what they feel has already happened. And they will encounter uncertainty by reproaching Freud's knowledge for being insufficient. More insufficiencies will follow and Freud will see these defenses as a repetition of infantile theories of learning, even as he readily admitted that their strange affair is the basis of and resource for anyone's imagination (Freud 1908).

Freud's lecture then shifts from his address to the general reader to practitioners of psychoanalysis. They are not left off the hook. The next resistance belongs to them and he warns that if they apply psychoanalysis only to others without questioning how they, too, are affected, two mistakes will follow. If the analyst insists that knowledge taken in is the same knowledge the analyst intends it to be, then psychoanalysis will dissipate into the uselessness of suggestion. Teaching and learning, like theory and practice, Freud argued, are by their nature in conflict with one another. If one tries to settle their discord, psychoanalysis will be lost. The second mistake occurs if the analyst imagines that only others have an unconscious and thus acts as if her interpretation only has to do with the analysand and not the countertransference. Psychoanalysis, Freud reminds both friend and foe, will affect the analyst in ways the analyst cannot control but nonetheless experiences. These two mistakes—that there is such a thing as transparent communication with an unequivocal language, and that the unconscious can be mastered—are defenses against being affected by the uncertainties of life that psychoanalysis invites us to put into words. The resistance, however, comes in many forms and, in Freud's view, resistance breeds resistance to resistance and the very thought of having psychology to affect psychology will incur ontic confusion. More haste will be created from the haze of knowledge.

Winnicott (1996) invited such confusion in his lecture on some difficulties in learning psychology. The difficulties of its learning, he will suggest, cannot be separated from its teaching. This is a different take from Freud in that whereas Freud insisted on conflict between teaching and learning and so on the discord between theory and practice, Winnicott focused on the ambivalent use of this conflict, with the assumption that students both want and do not want this knowledge. He expected students would be ruthless with and without concern for the object of knowledge and in this attack repeat what must remain as infantile in learning. Yet this aggressive move was not considered as resistance to the knowledge. In a curious way, he considered this aggression as a sign of hope that the object will survive. Winnicott does warn students that their first encounter with psychology will be affected; indeed, their destructive impulse will become an omnipotent defense. Students will measure this new knowledge against their own experience. If it does not hold up, then the knowledge cannot be believed. This reversed empathy will only lead to the analyst's mistake Freud mentioned: they may decide that the knowledge of psychology is only relevant to others who need it.

Where Winnicott departs from Freud is with a new question: will the knowledge survive the ruthlessness of object relating? If it does, these students may consider psychology as something to take in even if it is already there. This is just the beginning, for in taking in knowledge, our procedures of incorporation create whole new worlds in competition with the one already there. So his lecture concludes with a style of teaching and learning contained in the uncertain idea that even if we can take in the fact that our lives are first and foremost psychological lives lived with others and that our procedures made for trying to know will use new knowledge to repeat an archaic vulnerability of helplessness and defenses against it, we are left with the next affected question: what can one do with this new conviction that one's own psychology matters to how psychology can matter at all?

Both of these lectures by Winnicott and Freud attempted to warn us that psychology is our nervous condition. We will feel intruded upon by our own self-consciousness and cannot prevent our play of interiority from registering a protest against this gray matter. Yet the knowledge itself may make our nerves stand on end. Meltzer's (1992) discussion on claustrophobia gives us a clue as to why this may be the case: "psychoanalysis has moved relentlessly from a simplistic explanatory hypothesis and an optimistic aim to cure mental illness, towards a state of bewildered description of mental phenomena" (3). Our descriptions of mental life bewilder because mental life itself is bewildering. But this then means that knowledge will always be partial, contradictory, equivocal, and a transfer point.

Adorno (2006), as well, gave some lectures on psychology with a focus on the bewildered mind, what he saw as a mind under a spell of a social haze. Around that same time, Adorno (2007) recorded a dream about a lecture. In the dream a psychotherapist was giving a lecture on the music of Schubert, but from his field's psychological perspective. Adorno was in the audience. Suddenly, the lecture hall turned into a pub. A pianist was banging on the piano. Off-key, the psychotherapist began to sing a line from the Schubert lieder, titled "Impatience": "I would like to carve it on every tree-trunk" (69). In the dream Adorno became livid. He recorded what happened next: "I harangued [the audience] . . . with the argument that this performance was so barbaric that it turned anyone who tolerated it into a barbarian as well. . . . We all joined forces to beat the psychotherapist to death" (69). I imagine Adorno woke up in a mess; one could safely surmise that he didn't like therapists or, at the very least, didn't want to be mistaken for one even as he found himself giving lectures on psychology and working as an accidental psychologist (Hullot-Kentor 2006).

Without his associations, the dream cannot be interpreted. But enough is known about Adorno to point out that he loved his Schubert and saw in music the capacity to represent what cannot be met with reason but nonetheless urged its possibilities to feel what life can become. Yet the dream seems to doubt this radical hope. Moreover, the affects of the dream—outrage, impatience, haranguing, banging, carving, beating—lead to my speculation on his anger at lecturing on psychology: his feeling that he was in the wrong field that ruins the sublime or wishes to do so; his question as to whether he or his students would be as thick as wood and be barred from meaning; his impatience in the lecture; and, perhaps, his worry that somehow a therapist sitting in his lecture will judge him as a barbarian, just as he judged the therapist. Adorno, after all, had his quest in the intolerable and the traumatic. And so it can turn out that giving a lecture on psychology makes the lecturer dream.

My identification with this dream as well is emblematic of my anxious lectures on psychology: that I, too, will be seen by others as eschewing the material world, that I speak off-key the psychological register, that I'm taking cover in my own self-absorption, and that my speculations in psychology ruin the sublime of critical theory. I, too, worry that my lectures will be an episode of runaway meaning: a harangue instead of a hope. After all, when we plead for psychology, we are really pleading for ourselves and that certainly makes us nervous.

Adorno's (2006) lecture on psychology can be read as an elaboration of the affective side of learning psychology with his attempt to convey what is bewildering about having to live in a world others have already made. Like Freud and Winnicott, he begins with the ego defenses, also knowing that his students may ignore what he has to say when he reminds them of our character masks, itself a concept that has gone out of date or has been supplanted by identity claims. "By character masks I mean that while we imagine that we act as ourselves, in reality we act to a great extent on the agents of our own functions" (69). When we believe we are the authors of our origins and intentions, our egos mistake reason for being. Adorno then argues that, for any action to be possible at all, there must be something besides consciousness that urges it to act. He calls this impulse "the additional factor" (218) and later in the lecture links this impulse to act to " the corporal element, the very thing that cannot be fully identified with reason" (238).

Adorno was worried about something that is not reason, but cannot be separated from it. His lecture on psychology is really about the limits of imagination and its confusion of compliance to culture with its own self-preservation that is then fused to the desire to dominate nature, in turn becoming our second nature. And he attempts to warn these students about what they cannot help doing: mistaking their ego defenses with their character, missing how it is that the desire to dominate one's own nature turns against the self. Only here does he call upon psychoanalysis, with Anna Freud's (1995) discussion of the ego's defense of identification with the aggressor. The problem with identification with the aggressor, he says, is not so much that evil others are identified with and thus incorporated into ego, itself a terrible confusion of good and bad. Rather, for Adorno, the devastating identification is with "the course of the world just as it happens to be" (76). Through identifying with institutions, education, the law, the culture industry, or even the idea of progress, he says, we are not just subject to ideology but actually become ideology. This is what Adorno meant when he lamented the ways we become functions of our functions. No doubt, Adorno argues, humans are symbol-dependent creatures; we must think ourselves into being the authors of our consciousness and our freedom. The danger is that we forget not only our dependency on symbols but on others as well. And he suggests that if we mis-take the work of interpretation with the force of this immediate world, we may believe we accompany our representations, but, in actuality, cannot feel or think them as such.

One way to understand the collapse Adorno leaves us with is to turn to the problem of symbolization by considering "the additional factor," the bodily impulse that sets the mind to work, as anxiety. Klein (1930) proposed this bodily force as emerging from an instinct for knowledge, first dedicated to knowing and possessing the mother's insides and, later, this curiosity for what cannot be seen is transferred to the work of symbols. Its earliest form of knowledge, however, will be anxious and paranoid and will collapse from the pressure of its own concreteness, resulting in "symbolic equation" (220), where anxiety over loss is equated with an outside object. This is akin to what Adorno saw as mistaking the immediacy of the order of things for reality's test, a procedure that bewilders the problem of how the loss of the object's autonomy is also our loss of the object's representational, metaphori-cal, and even enigmatic qualities. In symbolic equation, nothing can change because phantasy and reality merge through the archaic defense of projective identifications.

The psychological paradox is that symbolization emerges from our earli-est efforts to know and thus both contains and conveys anxiety. André Green (2000), for example, argues that the work of symbolization requires a double action: a unity is attempted between two things that were split off and the new representation contains rather than disavows its earlier history of disunity and conflict. This view is close to how Adorno (2006) thinks of the function of art: as " a particular relation to the experience of structures that purport to be meaningful and that provide a model both of meaning that can be explored and of the crisis of meaning" (125).

These views on the symbolization take us to the heart of what is difficult about our psychology: we must symbolize affect and yet, according to Green's (1999) study on the status of affect, psychoanalysis puts forward the idea of a constitutive force-relation between affect and thought:

> If the affect is the witness of wild, ineliminable thought, present at the very heart of the most abstract, the most rational processes, the final refuge of the affect is rationalization. The fact that nothing, neither in its content nor in its form, allows us to distinguish it from reason, shows that the only attitude that it ought to inspire would be to let the discourse continue, until such time as its own movement, the one that forges it, undergoes the test of its challenge. (231)

In this sense, symbolization is our reality test for our desire for discourse to be affected. Affect's reason marks, propels, and leaves its remainder in every thought.

What is noteworthy in these lectures and in Adorno's strange dream is that symbolization contains the problem of negativity or destruction and so highlights the disunity, or the negative dialect carried on by our psychology and that migrates into meaning as such. And these affective processes already carried into meaning by the other begin our psychology and our attempts to think it. But this then means, to draw upon a Kleinian frame, that the work of integration is not a problem of continuity thought to guarantee the future but, rather, signifies the act of tolerating the disunity, nonsemblance, and the enigma of our subjectivity. Klein considers this work as ongoing and configured through depressive anxiety, an awareness of both the play of aggression and goodness in the process of trying to learn. If symbolization leans on what Klein (1935, 1940) came to understand as the depressive position—a toleration of absence and transience—then learning itself is also characterized by the work of mourning painful losses, including mourning the history of our disunity, what inhibits, fragments, or destroys the mind, and times when goodness seemed destroyed. These emotional processes are also the hallmark of a constitutive loneliness representation brings and that our symbolization inherits for commentary. This is also what Adorno understands as the function of art. A turn to the *Zeitroman*, or novels of disillusionment, critical of their age, will allow us to press this gray matter into the shape of the depressive position.

ZEITROMAN

Hans Castorp, our protagonist in *The Magic Mountain,* was twenty-three years old when he traveled from Hamburg to the International Sanatorium Berghof to visit his ill cousin. He planned to stay for three weeks and then return from his visit exactly as he had left. Except that on the day of his departure he came down with a cold, a fever, a pounding heart, and "a moist spot." The director, Behrens, advised him to stay on for an indeterminate amount of time and live like his ill cousin: take rest cures, walk, eat many meals each day, talk with the other patients, and attend lectures on unsanctioned love by the psychoanalyst Krokowski. Hans comes under the sway of many teachers, one of whom was the autodidact Settembrini involved in writing an endless encyclopedia on the topic of suffering and its cures that had the ambiguous title *Sociological Pathology.* Days blend into one another, the late nineteenth-century crept to its early twentieth, and time lost its efficiency. In no time at all, seven years will have passed. And our Hans will have been changed. On this Magic Mountain, Hans Castorp learns how to be ill by falling in love with an unattainable woman, Frau Clavdia Chauchat. This would be a world where something that got on his nerves, such as a woman's arm slamming the dining room door each time she entered, would become the cause of his love. Just as the slamming of the door carried meanings it never intended, so, too, did his pounding heart. Among other things, our *Zeitroman* symbolizes the inevitability of meaning's slips: that a pounding heart can mean a problem of the heart, fear, overexertion, desire, and sexual excitement and that the heart registers what the ear can hear and the eyes can see.

The omnipotent narrator of *The Magic Mountain*, the one critical of his age, warns us readers not to read for the novel's plot, partly because nothing much happens at the manifest level of this novel of ideas and because anticipating how they would come to matter before their time would be useless. There are other reasons to turn the page. But readers also learn to experience the pleasure of reading along with Hans who must first surrender to the Magic Mountain in order to feel what he thinks. It is not easy for Hans or us readers; only gradually do we learn to become a patient. As for Hans, he must first get his X-ray so that he can see for himself his "moist spot." The title of this chapter is "My God, I See It!" When Hans is made witness to the inside of his own hand, he feels something other than its gray matter: he realized that he would die. Seeing his insides leads to the thought of their loss. The director noticed his distress and said, "Spooky, isn't it? Yes, there's no mistaking that whiff of spookiness" (260).

Thoughts on the inevitability of his own death led him to do some research, without really knowing where his drive to know would lead him next. In the chapter titled "Research," Hans pores over scientific texts and in the attempt to make sense of his own insides bumped into the idea that these scientific and philosophical representations of the mind obscure their own procedures of representation. The novel's narrator, like a Greek chorus, registered Hans's anxiety with their repeated refrain: "What was life? No one knew" (326). As Hans continued to read and question life's ultimate meaning, he became aware of warmth spreading throughout his own body. Then, both his sensuality and his thoughts strayed into a dream.

Our narrator intrudes on Hans's reverie: "And yet for all that the accomplishments of protoplasm remained quite inexplicable—it seemed that life was prohibited from understanding itself" (334). Perhaps this prohibition lead Hans to transgress it by multiplying his surface: "at the very moment when one thought one had reached the outermost edge, everything began all over again . . . inner world after inner world within his own nature he was present over and over again—a hundred young Hans Castorps" (338). Hans exhausted himself with what Adorno spoke of as "the additional factor," that bodily impulse, that cannot comprehend itself yet creates a dream. In that unworldly world of dreams, research is symbolically equated with our first sexual research and our wishes for that knowledge of origin. Hans dreams that the arms of Frau Clavdia Chauchat, the very ones that kept slamming the dining room door, now wrap around him. Without reason, through the trial of acknowledging his own mortality, Hans finds love, itself a radical hope.

Things did not go as well for Gerald Weber, our fifty-five-year-old protagonist in Powers's novel *The Echo Maker*. He used to think of himself as a successful neurophysiologist and self-proclaimed specialist in presenting to the lay audience the field's case studies. With lectures, Weber proffered this knowledge as both cautionary tales of what can go wrong with the brain and as laudatory reports from the field on the progress of his science. In our age of research ethics, however, the public turns against Weber. He's accused of exploiting other people's narratives and violating their privacy. His colleagues have also turned against him. They consider his narrative approach as too soft, too subjective, filled with errors of desire. Weber feels himself as imposter, "the pseudoempirical equivalent of reality television, profiting from fad and pain" (222). Suddenly, Weber becomes stupid in academic conferences. When interviewed on television he feels speechless or worries that he sounds crazy. Is he promoting his own madness? Then, he worries these interviews will endlessly replay on the World Wide Web for all to see. He finds himself obsessively checking the Web, finding what he abhors, but not being able to stop looking for copies of himself and then chasing after his runaway identity.

Much of the novel concerns Weber's involvement with a special case of a young man with a brain injury and his sister Karin who left her own life to care for her brother. It was Karin who contacted Weber for help just at the point when he needed a new project. Mark Schluter cannot recognize his sister as his sister. Instead, he becomes more and more certain that she is a copy of his sister pretending to be his sister for some sinister purpose. Capgras syndrome is the name given to individuals who are certain that the most important and loved people in their lives are impostures or doubles pretending to be an original. Here the problem of giving birth to oneself reaches the height of its agony. Weber's increasing helplessness, indeed his susceptibility to the Capgras syndrome and to his own narrative impulse, forms the heart of the novel; what breaks the heart or stops it short revolves around how knowledge becomes, for all involved, both a reminder of absence and a transference car-nival. The irony is that throughout his adult life Gerald Weber has dedicated himself to explaining the minds of others without giving much thought to his own.

Late in the novel, Weber returns to the classroom for a lecture on the disorders of the mind, but his own thoughts intrude and criticize his efforts. The students, tattooed and pierced, now appear to him as foreign and hostile. He feels out of context. Just as his colleagues did, these students seemed to be waiting for him to make a mistake. In this transference, Weber can no longer tell the difference between what he sees and what he feels. And this transfer-ence intrudes, affecting perception and ruining his knowledge. He cannot tell the difference anymore between science and story. Our omnipotent narrator gives us this sense: "He cast a last look at his notes: organized ignorance, next to the brain, all human knowledge was like a lemon drop next to the sun" (359). Yet it is Weber who is melting. In an effort to save himself, he decides the only way to capture his students' attention would be to present the side-show of neuroscience, defending his efforts with the field's unpronounceable words. And even as he spoke of its famous cases, he felt ill, believing he saw his wife enter the lecture hall, but now as she was at age twenty-five. His jokes fell flat; the students were too young to have any associations. All he could do was describe how neurons became lost. Then he ran out of time. And just as Castorp had to confront the idea that no one knew, so, too, did Weber: "Long after his science delivered a comprehensive theory of self, no one would be a single step closer to knowing what it meant to be another. Neurology would never grasp from without a thing that existed only deep in the impenetrable inside" (365).

The students never knew what disaster occurred in Weber as he lectured them because they were having their own. Weber was beside himself; he was taken over by the young woman sitting in the lecture hall's back row whom he thought was his wife and whom he suddenly needed to have just as she walked away. In the midst of this mess, one of the hostile students then appeared to ask Weber about the case of David. "'Your account of that, that meningioma. David?' His voice apologized. Weber nodded him on. 'I'm wondering . . . I think that maybe my father. . . .'" (366). Weber had already stopped listening because he could not stop could looking for his wife, as she was when they first fell in love. He should leave teaching, he thought; maybe even write a neuroscience novel. And when Weber finally returned home that night and was asked by his wife how the lecture went, he replied that he was sure that he was brilliant, a way for him not to tell her how lost he had become.

Our protagonists have stumbled into the inadvertency of knowledge: it cannot provide its own reasons, protect itself from its equivocations and from our questions, and anticipate that which undoes it even as it undoes something else. But that then leaves us with our use of knowledge, however equivocal, as leaning on and conveyed through what Adorno called "the additional factor," a feeling that sets knowledge on edge with something that is not knowledge at all. This encounter, which feels more like a confrontation, is what Aulagnier (2001) proposed as "man's *factum* . . . the effect of anticipation" (10). We are always being confronted with the anxiety of not knowing and needing to know.

The critique of reason, too, has its remainder, for if reason is to reflect upon itself, if reason could see in itself the kernel of its madness, it may end in expectations of hopelessness. Against all odds, Adorno, with his additional factor—the idea that we can grow so sick of the order of things that we decide to say no to its demands and go a different way without really knowing what will happen next—suggests critical theory's depressive position. Hullot-Kentor's (2006) discussion of Adorno's work illustrates its paradox when he quotes his translation of a transcribed conversation between Adorno and his friend and coauthor, Horkheimer. Their insistence on a negative critique led Horkheimer to ask Adorno: "Can one really do anything with these sorts of ideas? My difficulty is that I always get exactly as far as we have gotten today, that is, as far as objective despair." Adorno replied, "What gives knowledge the stamp of authenticity is the reflection of possibility" (30). This did not seem to satisfy Horkheimer so he tried again with what he felt he lost in objective despair:

> HORKHEIMER: I have not given up the claim to happiness, but I do not believe in happiness. Whoever really believes in happiness is in the worst sense naïve.
>
> ADORNO: We must be at once more naïve and much less naïve. (30)

One could argue that there is no such thing as objective despair because the experience of despair leads to something that is both objective and subjective: loss, absence, and, perhaps, resignation. And, even in despair, one cannot stop wanting something more.

RADICAL HOPE

That psychology makes us nervous—by which I mean psychology as that affective index associating and writing the evocative meanings of life joined by our anticipations, phantasies, and expectations for the other—characterizes the vulnerability of learning. Even if symbolization can never complete our desire, our libidinal world founders without its work. Klein (1940) proposed this work as the depressive position, where the inevitable losses that compose and decompose life constitute not only the sadness of its learning that revives our constitutive loneliness but, more centrally, she saw the potential for love, gratitude, reparation, and symbolization as emerging from human loss. Animated by the other's absence, the depressive position urges the symbolization of this gray matter of knowledge, now as residue, association, and remainder. It is a style of conveying self-knowledge as much as it is an experience with learning knowledge beyond the self.

Lear's (2006) discussion of radical hope may be read as urging a new consideration of the depressive position when he describes one of the profound limits of consciousness: it cannot prepare for its own destruction and for the destruction of its telos. In some sense, Lear's view of radical hope goes beyond the depressive position, for its potential can only be felt from the ruins of identity, reason, and cultural life, when every working assumption of how the world should be is no longer meaningful, available, or relevant. Yet the paradox is that culture designs our continuity. Its pedagogical efforts organize continuity between generations secured through cathexis of rituals and categories of cognition, mimesis, and recognition, through modes of childrearing, and through outlets for sexuality and aggression. Through its conceptual categories of intelligibility, beauty, and truth and with its group psychology and its definitions of madness and sanity, culture's propositions of what counts as success and failure depend on the presumption of continuity. Ontological vulnerability, however, disrupts its plans, as does the problem of language itself. Things can always mean something other than what is pronounced and we are subject to our overhearing. Yet the defenses needed to split off vulnerability from its own nature cannot maintain themselves for the simple reason that culture is also the repository for our love, our reality, and our Weltanschauung, all humanly created things that break (Bass 1998). Even if the mind is a plastic mind, its creations—desire, meaning, goodness, and love—are all subject to loss. Because efforts in continuity cannot anticipate or imagine its own disunity, culture, as with consciousness, contains within its own design its breaking point. Its nature is to resist its own plasticity, its own excess.

Anthropologists have taught us that, for cultures to persist, they must be capable of extreme, radical change at the level of their most intimate symbolization. Humans must, if they are to live, meet this same demand. But this demand for symbolizing that which does not exist can be felt as persecution and then be symbolically equated with loss of unity, purpose, and reason. The paradox is that culture and consciousness, and the educational structures that render them intelligible, given their intention of mastering nature, lose their pliability in order to be plausible. Lear tells us that, for radical change to occur, culture and consciousness must give up and leave behind all that was once relevant to living a life. I believe this surrender characterizes the depressive position and the psychological qualities of teaching and learning.

Without guarantee, Lear proposes a new ethic in the form of "a commitment to the idea that the goodness of the world transcends one's limited and vulnerable attempts to understand it . . . no claim to grasp ineffable truths" (95). Lear suggests that the resource for radical hope—the hope that something good, even as one cannot know in advance what form goodness will take—flowers within what is enigmatic to both consciousness and culture, what it does not yet know. Dreams, as a creative play on affected reality, are one enigmatic resource because they invite interpretation and imagination. Literary knowledge, a knowledge that cannot be in charge of itself and that can set meaning loose without knowing its destination, is another.

When Lear writes of radical hope, he ties it to the fact that we are "finite erotic creatures" (119), another way of proposing our depressive position. This was a fact that Hans Castorp confronted, that the neurophysiologist eventually came to ponder, and that our lecturers Freud, Winnicott, and Adorno attempted to convey. We may imagine our omnipotence, but cannot be omnipotent. We may project ourselves into the world and mistake our identifications for perceptions, yet this can only be the beginning. We creatures are slow learners, subject to risks, mistakes, errors, misjudgments, and unhappiness, dependent as we are on the mismatch of self and other. Even as we project ourselves into the world to identify with it and even with our additional factor of anxiety, all of which lends meaning and enigma to our erotic character, the world is more than our finite projections. But the problem of telos is also a problem of our psychology. In Lear's view: "It is because of our finite, erotic natures that we come to conceive of ourselves as finite erotic creatures" (123). I add to that our additional factor perhaps best described as the drive. It takes a psychology to make a psychology, and because of this gray matter, we can come to symbolize ourselves as finite, erotic beings with all the naivete, disunity, hope, and desire it brings. For these reasons, learning and teaching psychology take us beyond psychology.

CHAPTER FIVE

COUNTERTRANSFERENCE

═══════════════════

Unless we take into account our nurseries and our family homes,
our behaviour to our schoolmasters would be not only incompre-
hensible but inexcusable.

—Sigmund Freud, "Some Reflections on a Schoolboy Psychology"

Most teachers agree that the act of teaching conveys more than the material
taught. We run into trouble, however, if that something is attributed to "the
unconscious." More often than not, we do not want to know anything about
it. So the idea that teaching transfers the teacher's emotional world (including
what is unconscious about it) as much as it does the material may be hard to
take sitting down, for it means that, in teaching, each and every aspect of the
self, including its most unwanted and unknown parts, is called upon. The idea
that the teacher communicates something she knows nothing about invites
our passion for ignorance. When Freud (1914b) wrote of his schoolboy years,
he admitted that he did not know which affected him more: what the teacher
taught or whom the teacher was like. He was fairly sure that teachers ignored
the students' emotional use of them, although on reading Freud's passionate
description, it seems odd to be so blind to this family romance:

> We courted them or turned our backs on them, we imagined sympathies
> and antipathies in them which probably had no existence, we studied their
> characters and on theirs we formed or misformed our own. They called up

our fiercest opposition and forced us to complete submission; we peered
into their little weaknesses, and took pride in their excellences, their knowledge and their justice. At bottom we felt a great affection for them if they
gave us any ground for it, though I cannot tell how many of them were
aware of this. (242)

The unconscious steps in precisely when we are not aware of it. We can
say with conviction that education emerges from the transference-love made
between the teacher and students. It takes its force from the emotional world
and that teachers' responses to how they are (unconsciously) addressed is the
basis for the teachers' quandaries, or the countertransference: feelings, phantasies, anxieties, defenses, and wishes made from what teaching feels like. But
why is it that what is most subjective in our work—the stuff that lends cre-
dence and incredulity to our conceptions of teaching and learning—is hardly
considered as the flora and fauna of our teaching practices? Can this subjective
world be used as an enigmatic resource for understanding the boundaries,
limits, and desires of subjects at work?

The problem made by denying the force and influence of the teacher's
emotional world is that if we cannot link how we feel to the way our work
conveys and transforms our feelings and ideas, both the work and the self are
diminished. If only seen as a technical skill, the language of teaching suffers
from what Gregorio Kohon (2007) calls "symbolic impoverishment" (212).
It becomes impossible to wonder how the work of the unconscious, itself an
index of our affective history of learning desire, leads us to what we look for
and hope to refind in the world of others. But it is as if this index is always
being written in invisible ink, referencing what is illegible in experience. We
must read between the lines for the advent and vicissitudes of our emotional
world; but, to do that, we need a language and an educational setting unafraid
to write a story different from the one anticipated.

My assumption is that the teacher's object relations—a way to characterize the affective workings of our inner world—are her earliest emissaries of
learning and give play to practices of teaching. Object relations personify
features of affect, turning them into feelings given perspectives from the vantage of their phantasies, anxieties, and their archaic psychological history.
They convey what is enigmatic about one's feelings toward others, instruct
and disrupt hopes for recognition, and rationalize disappointments. It is not
that object relations are little people in our head, although sometimes we
may depict our feelings as inner voices, as intuition, and as cautionary warning devices. Object relations always refer to events with someone. They are
formed from taking in features of others from the vantage of how others relate

and form relations with us and with their others. Object relations contain what is good and bad; we express these judgments through styles of loving and hating, through what we take in and expel, within what we assume as the incline and decline of knowledge, and then they service urges for destruction and reparation. They can be thought of as the procedures, functions, mechanisms, and theories of feelings. And they break through the barrier of conscious intention to convey what is enigmatic and unresolved about feelings of dependency, love, recognition, authority, and care.

The version of the human behind this theory is that, from our beginning, we are not merely dependent on others for our needs, but are object seeking and object making. In this view, the teacher's feelings represent a history of her learning object relations and gain semblance and disunity in the presence of teaching and learning. That teachers have grown up in school only to return as adults means that their relations to authority, knowledge, to school objects, and to the differences between the teacher and the student are never neutral but rather are in conflict with their own infantile phantasies of education, now in the form of implicit theories of learning and teaching and their idealization of the profession (Britzman 2003b). Yet this subjective aspect of the teacher's world also conveys what is most problematic about boundaries; it is one of our most difficult and avoided topics and perhaps the most delicate to interpret because feelings turn need into demand and then to desire. Feelings signify our relations to others: how we wish to encounter them, what it feels like to miss them, what we want from others without having to ask, and so on. Feelings get hurt, disguise themselves, are projected into others, return as identifications, and then set out again through projections. They muddle boundaries of time and space and of self and other. Feelings, as statements of need, are difficult to acknowledge and read.

So if we are object seeking, what can this mean for how we organize education and how we recognize what counts as pedagogical? If representation is a basic feature of psychic life, what is it like to symbolize our most intimate wishes? There does not seem to be an official engagement with affect's advent, no psychological language that structures the work of learning a profession and that is readily called upon to interpret the emotional meanings of the teacher's world and her sense of happening education. We have yet to construct a language for teachers' learning the work of education that invites curiosity toward interpreting their inner world and how it links to conceptualizations, symbolization, and interpretations of education. Over the course of this chapter, I suggest one word that may be of use in understanding what teaching feels like when the teacher is confronted with her or his boundaries, limits, and desire: the countertransference. As readers will see, the word carries its own difficulties because its meanings cannot be settled, because of the contentious history it holds in the education of psychoanalysis, and because getting to know one's feelings may also mean encountering emotional pain, hostility, and aggression. And these affects do break open the boundaries of the teacher's imaginary.

To be fair, it is not only the field of education that forecloses inquiry into the use of our emotional world; few institutions welcome our unanswerable questions and our need to symbolize our excitement and doubts in representation (Newcombe 2007). Few institutions have the means to address the emotional life they both call upon and may agonize with its rules, routines, and implicit cultural life. Yet education, whether for adults or children, plays a role unlike any other institution and so lends to teachers a particular responsibility for a world students have not made yet nonetheless inherit, represent, and affect. In the space of education, the promise of knowledge and language are given their promise by teachers' relations to their work and their difference from their students. That we have language at all, however, means a lifelong struggle to symbolize affect into feelings and to make from that admixture self-knowledge and relations to the world. Putting urges to words, feeling heard by the other, questioning one's motives, and being curious about what is on one's mind, is, after all, a sign of hope that language is more than a technical exercise of literal description that protects us from what is latent in our words, even if our meanings are congealed again by that which is there before us: the procedures of language and its means of repression. But language also returns us to a primary loss and, in straining to overhear, one experiences overmeaning, only to encounter what Aulagnier (2001) calls "the violence of interpretation." No one can read our minds, nor can we read the minds of others. As speaking subjects, we may be reminded of this loss as it bounces between the image and the word, the desire and having to say it to someone.

I believe to understand the depth and potent creativity of the emotional world requires a particular language dedicated to that world's symbolization, a language that can contain "the violence of interpretation" by attending to its own affective play, including aggression and scenes of love and hate. Some of its qualities would be to invoke the means to analyze its constructions, break open the claustrophobic space between the word and the thing, and, of course, be represented by speakers unafraid of their own negativity and the words used to name it. In short, I am suggesting an erotic language that attracts the speaker's interest and involvement in the play of interpretation and its rough edges, a language that can question its own work. Compare this view with the obfuscation, so ingrained that it almost goes without saying, of what is demanded of teachers: teachers love students and are altruistic, unstamped by narcissism. That such an insistence is developmentally impossible is almost beside the point. That it can be encountered as chastisement for the feelings one does hold may be this discourse's secret desire. This use of language does not so much keep us in line as it functions to draw the line between good and bad teachers.

We may attribute some of our affective chaos to the nature of what is human in the human professions. After all, education as an impossible profession relies on and bothers the subjectivity of its practitioners as much as it tries to wrest it away through knowledge of its procedures and functions and, paradoxically, with the education of educators. Are there other ways to account for the upset made when we try to make sense of what we feel should count as good and bad practice and its conceptions of being right and wrong? How are we to understand what one feels while thinking on one's feet? And, along with the immediacy of the felt encounter, how might we make sense of our afterthoughts, the ones that cast their doubts on the question of what counts as education and malediction? Rarely are these judgments of good and bad education considered as links to affect, to how one feels while one teaches, to why certain feelings render one's actions as hazy or crazy or to what it can mean to grow numb and depressed in our work. Even the sources of feelings themselves are hardly linked to the teacher's object relations and how her history of wishes, phantasies, anxieties, and defenses returns in the presence of teaching. The missing link is that the teacher's feelings are a theory of learning, but that this theory of learning is, more often than not, a residue of infantile education.

The field of education has plenty of terms to steer the teacher's actions away from her or his emotional life by reducing teaching to the mastery of the student's learning. We speak readily in the shorthand of behavioral goals and objectives, and of the teacher aims, purpose, and strategies for delivering lessons. We think of where students should be because of our efforts.[1] We can say that the language used to discuss the teacher's work, grounded in behavioral psychology, is an externalizing one, that it reduces teaching and learning to a problem of the student's reception to the teacher's efforts, and that it flattens our frustration to the condition of being endlessly irritated at the student who writes bad sentences, misspells words, and can't read anyway. The dry language of technical expertise, usually conflated with the teacher's experience, however, is not easily thought of as a defense against being affected by and with our work. We do not readily speak of the teacher's narcissistic injuries, or the use of archaic defenses of projective identification, omnipotence, and splitting. We do not often associate our demand for certainty in our work to the Kantian notion of empty thoughts,[2] or through the traumatic events Bion (1993b) called "an attack on linking" (93), the ways a thinker destroys her mind by severing thoughts from their affective ties and being frightened by new ideas.

The teacher's emotional life, as learning from experience, remains without words, without a language that invites curiosity toward her own learning and to what else happens when one works with others. And we hardly ask one another, what kind of teacher do you want to be? I believe these silences are devastating to the teacher's creativity and to the promise of education. To understand the gambles of our emotional world, I turn to the language of psychoanalysis, one of the few practices and theories in the human professions that begins with and is affected by the relation between our object world[3] and our sense of relationships with self, others, and knowledge. This psychoanalytic effort will bring together two different experiences of education: the analyst's education and the teacher's education. Comparing their education will take us into the heart of the problem of countertransference.

Throughout this chapter, I will be claiming that the teacher's world is first and foremost an affected world and representing its eventfulness lends new grounds for the teacher's learning. I consider that the teacher's psychical conflicts—affects conveyed through phantasy, anxieties, and defenses against them—provided that they can be symbolized, are an enigmatic resource for insight into the nature of teaching and learning and its play of object relations. I will also suggest that much of what occurs to the teacher emerges from the negation made within what Lacan (1998a) called "the passion for ignorance" (121), used to describe the teacher's imaginary history of education that includes not only instituted education but the family romance and infantile theories made in childhood. These archaic phantasies are called upon and unhinged from their first history and become one of the underpinnings of the teacher's countertransference. They return when, say, a new student feels terribly familiar, when the teacher feels the echoes of narcissistic injury, when the day goes badly, when the teacher just doesn't feel right but cannot anchor feelings with its reasoning, and when the teacher does not know but feels that she should. In all these affective events, the teacher's unconscious is animated without its being symbolized. Projected into the screen of education are the teacher's conflicts and identifications. The tension is that if these affects are deemed as only a disruption to the work, we forfeit the idea of how their tenacity breaks the heart of the teacher's learning.

In my view, what our field of education defends against when it disavows the teacher's affect is a problem best described as one of experiencing experience, by which I mean making sense of what is first felt as nonsense: the unexpected ways we become affected by what happens to us because of what we try to make happen. I am contrasting this view to the field's dictum of acquiring experience or being experienced, ideology that dismisses and even makes unthinkable the idea that experience is always emotional experience and as such always signifies frustration and resistance. A second aspect of the problem is that the psychology that has most influenced the teacher's education and the one that organizes education's structure is Skinnerian behaviorism with its emphasis on problems of motivation, stimulus and response, and the language of mastery. Behaviorism is an expedited theory of learning that presents with certainty the work of teaching as consisting in reinforcing student learning through the exchange of reward and punishment. It provides experience as necessity, not as contingency. Here, it is important to recall that humans are object seeking; our needs and wants are addresses to the other. We wish to be met. A third aspect of the problem resides not in our field's negations but within a constitutive difficulty of symbolizing the work of affect in the teacher's learning since this would take us into problems of representing the meaning of emotional pain made from the teacher's love and hate, pleasure and unpleasure, masochism and sadism, paranoia and obsessionality, and, too, the teacher's erotic life, for instance. It would take us into words that may at first be blamed for their meanings, as an indication of the "violence of interpretation."

The psychoanalyst Ester Bick (1987), who worked with teachers in their educational contexts, suggests that being with others is always an emotional experience made from conflating perception with one's own internal aggression and defenses against it:

> The greatest bar to protecting oneself or people whom one loves from the many external danger situations that arise, is the difficulty in disentangling those from other dangers deriving from one's own destructive impulses. The destructiveness from within is the one danger from which we can never escape—physically speaking it kills us all in the end—yet it is the danger which we spend much of our energy in trying to escape, to deny, and to project outwards. Insofar as we do this, it clouds our perception of ourselves and of our world. It causes us to be unduly fearful; to look for other people to blame; to take up positions of inferiority from which we can feel above reproach. (312)

I draw attention to Bick's discussion on anxiety to include the idea that a great deal of the work of teaching turns on the problem of loss: of love, of meaning, and of idealization. Fear of losing invokes the old feeling that something in our objects is dangerous. Bick reminds us we cannot flee from our objects, but we do evacuate them into others. In this cycle of situating blame, the idea that the teacher may be rehearsing and evacuating a history of her or his losses hardly comes to mind. What may be more difficult concerns the idea that the teacher's negativity may well be the basis of self-understanding.

The question of what emotions may mean for the teacher was raised over fifty years ago. The classic study of the teacher's emotional world is Arthur Jersild's (1955) *When Teachers Face Themselves*. Its title tells us the whole story in miniature, for when teachers face themselves they experience what is enigmatic and ineffable in their inner world, including the boundaries, temporality, and space of emotional life, and the difficult feelings that accompany any human relation. Today, we can situate this study as the beginning of the movement of humanistic education and its openness to student movements for civil rights, the Vietnam antiwar movement, the women's movement, the deschooling movement, and their grand narratives of feminism, black liberation, gay liberation, and children's liberation. But also, for a time in North America, these world crises of antiimperialism, liberation, education, and identity were thought through with educational innovation joined with the therapeutic ideas of people like Carl Rogers, Eric Fromm, Karen Horney, Martin Buber, Erik Erikson, and Anna Freud (Britzman 1998). Their views are worth recalling.

Their therapeutics of education spanned the life cycle. They insisted that conflicted emotional relationships, there from the beginning of life with others, are the first means for self-understanding and the capacity to think with others. They linked interest in the uncertainties of being with others to the fragile ground for learning. They all proposed a relation between observing the world and self-understanding. They were concerned with conceptualizing the emotional pain constituted by the difficulties of listening and dialogue, of choosing freedom, of understanding the meanings of presence and absence, and of the conflicts between the conscious and the unconscious. They wondered how these developmental fault lines affect our sense of mortality, morality, judgment, and ethics, and thought of these actions as emerging from and conveying emotional experience. Such concerns as these led them to create a therapeutic of self/other relations joined to education.

Jersild's study can now be read as anticipating these great educational changes when he asked teachers to question the significance of their emotional life. His method was a strange combination of Likert scale and phenomenology. Teachers were invited to contrast what people say with what they actually believed and thought, to identify the congealment of belief with compliance and discuss how compliance leans on hostility. He identified areas where teachers knew they parroted the fears and ideas of others even as they believed in something else. He tried to get at the secret thinking of teachers.[4] He placed emotional life in the discord of autonomy and dependency, which in turn structured his chapters on anxiety, loneliness and the search for meaning, and sex, hostility, and compassion. Jersild considered this vocabulary as central to the teacher's self-understanding. A great deal of this work included giving language to the arbitrary undertows of education, where suddenly the teacher feels taken over by the immediacy of experience, institutional demands, and feelings insufficiency.

Yet the undertow is more than the force of school structure, although this structure seems to pull us back to childhood conflicts with dependency and authority. Its force is also a metaphor for our drives, bodily impulses seeking objects, expressing aims, and exerting pressure. Jersild suggests there is something in the work of teaching that may call forth the teacher's hate, Eros, and frustration, for example. His study is also noteworthy for another reason: Jersild may have been the first educator to describe the unconscious world of the teacher and her ego defenses against that world. And the teachers he spoke with admitted that there was a great deal about their selves that they did not understand but would like to know more about. While the teachers and Jersild called this area of concern "self-understanding" (15), we can ask: what is the nature of the knowledge involved and what resists the Socratic commitment to "know thyself"? Further, how is it possible to think about self-understanding if the language of teaching obliterates the self who teaches when it demands that teachers need to be ultraistic and just serve the students.

Bick (1996) noticed a similar wish in child psychoanalysts. She divides internal stresses into "preformed anxieties" (169), or what the analyst brings into the profession, and countertransference issues, or how the analyst is affected by preformed anxieties and the child's conveyance of suffering. They are linked. She warns that while there are "real" problems the child faces, meaning external factors that impinge on the child's suffering, the analyst's feelings are also real. The problem is how preformed anxiety is used to rationalize away the feelings of the analyst as unimportant as compared to the external disaster of the child. Yet the analyst's feelings are an enigmatic resource of her work and one way to know this is because of the conflicts the work invites her to address:

> The intensity of the child's dependence, of his positive and negative transference, the primitive nature of his phantasies tend to arouse the analyst's

own unconscious anxieties. The violent and concrete projections of the
child into the analyst may be difficult to contain. Also the child's suffering
tends to evoke the analyst's parental feelings, which have to be controlled so
that the proper analytic role can be maintained. All these problems tend to
obscure the analyst's understanding and to increase in turn his anxiety and
guilt about his work. (171)

In Bick's account, the feelings of the analyst are tied to both the child and
to the analyst's own experience with the profession. And this intersubjectivity is conflicted, as all intersubjectivity must be. The analyst is subject to her
own anxiety and to the anxiety of the other. The other powerfully affects the
analyst's identifications, phantasies, and defenses, as do the myths of the work
itself and *countertransference* is the term given over to this relation. As the analyst
was once a child, she brings to the work the many irresolvable conflicts being
a child leaves behind. These conflicts, however, are not so out of reach that
they cannot be called back in times of current distress. The analyst's regression
is a risk of the work yet, without the capacity to regress, the analyst would be
hard-pressed to understand the child. It is an awareness of these unconscious
relations that may characterize the ways the psychoanalyst's work comes into
being. I believe the educator steps into a similar mine field: anxieties and guilt
over the nature of their work, fears of regression, and feelings of helplessness
and parental identifications.

THE CANDIDATE ANALYST AND THE TEACHER

I am both a university professor and a candidate training in a psychoanalytic
institute. As a try to learn another impossible profession and as my psychoanalytic training unfolds, I am reminded of my time of learning to teach, when I
had to return to high school as a student teacher. It was chaotic and unnerv-
ing; the learning was painful, made from dreaded experiences of mistakes,
misunderstandings, and missteps and then having to learn to understand my
feelings as a way back into my teaching. At the time, it felt like too much to
ask since I was learning before I could understand and I did not understand
the swirl of my own emotional life, let alone the emotional world of others.
There was no way to prepare for the strange time of learning's deferral and no
protection from the emotional pain of experience. I am also reminded of my
conflictive hopes for educational change and the education I wish for. While I
want to believe that my psychoanalytic training is making me a better teacher
and that my background in teaching allows creativity in my psychoanalytic
work, more often than not I am confronted with the surprising question:

what kind of learner will I be? I could hardly prepare for feeling again like a bad student, for the bitter fights with my classmates, for not really understanding the hatred I made, and for barely containing my elaborate fantasies of revenge against whomever I believed was in my way. What I did not anticipate is how these familiar object relations configure my countertransference to both education and to learning.

Here, too, the training requires my emotional presence, yet I have difficulty in the seminars analyzing my feelings while trying to learn with others. Is there something about the nature of education itself that returns to us our deepest fears and wishes and to our earliest learning of love and hate? And if the experience of education is other to the structure of education and if learning conflicts are the inevitable consequence of this mismatch, what would it be for education to begin with or even notice its own contribution to what is also a conflict needed for learning to become something more than a repetition of one's childhood of education? Can education renew its promise for the promise of language and knowledge?

In returning to school as a student, I find myself flummoxed by its arbitrary rules, by meeting teachers I do not like, by the dependency the educational structure seems to invite and disavow, by having to follow directions, and by feeling subject to my childhood of education. It is difficult to separate who is doing what to whom. I am struck by how helpless I feel in my learning and how easily I regress to my adolescent defenses of idealization. My hope for an educational oasis and perhaps what may be a wish for an oceanic education without pain now seems like I've returned to narcissism and all of the defenses this entails. I'll return to these conflicts in my "tailpiece,"[5] with the idea that there is no smooth transition between education and learning, between intellectual understanding and affective insight, and no smooth transition between the fields of education and psychoanalysis. Indeed, these conflicts *are* the education and symbolizing them is the work one learns with the help of a language to understand what is loved and hated about learning.

My idea is that the training of analysts has a great deal in common with the education of teachers because both fields invite the childhood of education and the subjectivity of the practitioners. Both professions experience the conflict between theory and practice, encounter others as the objects of their practice, are supervised by others in one's work, write reports, attend conferences, and, at least ideally, consider their education as ongoing. Both groups study in educational institutes and so are subject to both their childhood theories of learning and to the institute's implicit theories of learning a profession that itself is subject to the dream of education. There are some significant differences in the respective education: the largest is that the analyst under-goes her own analysis, undergoes analytic treatment and is a patient. It is here, rather than in the didactic seminars of psychoanalytic training, that one may confront the truth of trying to learn and where one may interpret infantile strategies of learning, one's own unconscious theories. It may strike those of us in education as odd to take this quality of training into our field; that is, to require teachers to undergo a psychoanalysis to qualify as teachers. After all, how would this be graded? Anna Freud (1974), for instance, made this argument that teachers be analyzed and I believe it is useful to reconsider the nature of this request—what it would ask of teachers in their own learning—since self-analysis only comes after an analysis with others.

The other differences between these fields can be best approached through how psychoanalysis thinks about the way its work unfolds as in relationship with the analyst's unconscious. Fernando Urribarri (2007) poses this as a prob-lem of language and listening: "The acknowledgement that the unconscious "speaks" in many dialects promotes an ideal of a 'polyglot analyst'" (184). But here, too, in learning a language that speaks more than it can say, and that can say the opposite of what it means, psychoanalysis may find its limit in how it thinks about its own education. The differences between learning to teach and learning to be an analyst founders on the paradox of education: while one finds in psychoanalytic training an orientation to clinical practice and a rich vocabulary for this scene to play, the emotional experience of learning this work is felt as a private matter and is difficult to symbolize. It is almost as if the power of psychoanalysis would break open the silences of its own education, which leads me to think that psychoanalytic institutes might stretch Anna Freud's view to analyze their educational structures.

Within psychoanalytic work, there are four qualities of practice that could be useful for imagining educational relations and the structure of education, whether it is the education of teachers or of psychoanalysts. First, one finds in psychoanalytic discussions attention to the analyst's and the analysand's emo-tional contribution to the therapeutic work. That is, there is the idea that, in the clinic of psychoanalytic practice, the analyst and the analysand create together, through the slow work of construction, the psychoanalytic objects both will use and destroy over the course of the treatment. Their respective positions and different functions mean that understanding is always under construction and repair. Second, the analyst's feelings in this work are subject to further analysis and are considered as a reservoir of information. The work itself is to clarify, in terms that tolerate frustrated satisfaction, experiences when clarity eludes the analyst. Only gradually does the analyst learn to work from within this ignorance without leaning on a passion for ignorance or the stance of not wanting to know anything about it. Third, there is an attention to the analyst's function, or the asymmetrical responsibilities of the analyst and the analysand. As part of the analyst's work, the analyst learns to analyze her practices as consisting of and opening her motivations, defenses, fears, phantasies, and disclaimed experiences. These great unknowns are considered as both a needed resource for understanding the work and what destroys it. And fourth, there is the cultivation of an awareness of not knowing and an ethic of tolerating this uncertainty as part of what the analyst learns over and over. But this means that the place of both theory and practice repeats these odds.

If these psychoanalytic orientations can structure the educational encounter as well—that teachers and students create the objects of learning, that there is a difference in their respective roles, that tolerating not knowing allows the work of learning to proceed, and that the analysis of one's experience is the teacher's significant learning—then education may be in contact with its unconscious emotional scenery. It is after the event of teaching that the teacher's work can symbolize the question of what becomes of education. While there are many words to describe these affective relations, in what follows, I confine my comments to the work of the countertransference, keeping in mind that what links education and psychoanalysis is a theory of learning.

COUNTERTRANSFERENCE

The idea of countertransference is one way to conceptualize both how the analyst is unconsciously influenced by feelings the work creates and the consequences of these feelings for the analyst's capacity to think about psychoanalytic work and her or his analytic function. The term underlines the idea that the analyst is susceptible, affected by the dynamics, conflicts, and functions of psychoanalytic contact and that being affected can be thought of as an enigmatic resource for the work. The tension is that self-understanding is constructed by considering the other's influence as an emotional experience with ideas, associations, and theories of life. So countertransference is both a technical frame and a danger. The term has a rich and conflictive history in psychoanalysis and while it is well beyond this chapter to index its many meanings, including how this term may perform the history of psychoanalysis itself, a few discussions may be useful to thinking about the teacher's emotional dilemmas. Its transformations in meaning and in use give us a clue as to how combustible its theoretical problematic is for both the analyst and the analysand.

In a rather polemic address early on in the psychoanalytic movement, Freud (1910) argued that countertransference indicates the unresolved feelings of the analyst that are given free play under the guise of treating the patient. It was akin to the analyst's acting out without an ulterior motive but with an intuitive defense. When something feels right, there is the countertransference that Freud felt destroyed the analyst's neutrality and free-floating attention. Freud believed that the analyst's susceptibility to the analysand's influence was a consequence of the analyst's own unresolved complexes and so the countertransference really belonged only to the psychical conflicts of the analyst. Something happens to the one who gives help and who may feel helplessness when doing so. And while Freud knew the analyst must be affected to do her or his work, must have a conviction about the power of unconscious communication, when it comes to the transference-love, the analyst's countertransference needs to be analyzed, not enacted.

One large question is from where does the countertransference come? Does the patient project her feelings into the analyst who then plays out a particular role? Are the analyst's feelings already there and so ready at hand? Perhaps, given the asymmetric mutuality of the analytic session, countertransference is a new construction? Or, it really is difficult to say who is doing what to whom when two unconscious subjects meet. In the early history of psychoanalysis, however, Freud urged the analyst to the procedures of self-analysis as a means to overcome the countertransference feelings. Here, the countertransference was deemed an obstacle to the analyst's neutrality and an indicator of his emotional fragility.[6]

Benjamin Wolstein's (1988) introduction to his edited volume on the transformations of the uses and meanings of countertransference points to the key problem Freud opened when the countertransference was only seen from the perspective of the technical failing of the analyst. Wolstein reminds his readers that the origin of psychoanalysis began with Freud's exploration of his own psychical life, essentially his own transferences by interpreting his dreams and his symptoms as meaningful to self-understanding. Many consider that Freud's transference of his psychical events into a theory of psychical life lends to psychoanalysis its potential humanity. This leads Wolstein to raise the significant question: why not take as a model, and as the basis of psychoanalytic technique, Freud's creative process of self-analysis? It is this question that touches the analyst's education. Why not begin with the work of the dreamer? Or, why not take the analytic session as a dream?

In one of the more extensive surveys, Heinrich Racker (2002) argues that countertransference is best understood as the analyst's total psychological response made within the analyst's "intention to understand" (135) her or his patient. This does not seem to settle much because two unconscious subjects occupy and meet in the analytic setting and each has a history of trying to understand and be understood. Indeed, the intention to understand is already an emotionally wrought experience, for it returns us to times when we cannot understand and when we ourselves feel misunderstood. This is the history that composes the countertransference configuration. But the question countertransference poses is different from the question of empathy in that in empathic efforts one tries to understand the emotional logic of the other from that vantage whereas, in countertransference, the analyst may identify with the analysand's internal objects in such a way that her own internal conflicts repeat the analysand's pain (Bolognini 2001). What can play out then are the phantasies of lost understandings.

Racker suggests that the psychoanalytic process relies on the analyst's Eros, a particular orientation to listening, to relating, to interpreting, and to being silent. He goes so far as to say that understanding itself is Eros: "It is, above all, the understanding of what is rejected, of what is feared and hated in the human being, and this thanks to a greater fighting strength, a greater *aggression*, against which conceals the truth against illusion and denial—in other words, against man's fear and hate toward himself, and their pathological consequences" (32). I find Racker's formulation sufficiently dramatic since he includes the carnival of affects that provoke and destroy the need to understand: love, hate, fear, envy, aggression, and how these affects are evaded and disclaimed. These missed experiences, felt before they are known, must be symbolized to confront what is most existential and most fragile about our lives. Indeed, therapeutic action depends on the analyst's Eros, a desire the analyst must put into action in order to urge the other's desire. But this introduces the analyst's difference, how the analyst understands and so sets into motion "the violence of interpretation" by which I mean the idea that language comes at a terrible price in that it names the absence and animates loss of the object.

James Strachey (1990) eventually ties an understanding of therapeutic action to the analyst's difficulty in giving mutative interpretations, by which he means an interpretation that opens thinking to the force of its emotional meanings. He suggests that analysts have all sorts of reasons for not giving interpretations and then draws upon Klein's views: "Mrs. Klein has suggested to me that there must be some quite special internal difficulty to be overcome by the analyst in giving interpretations" (76). While not explicitly linking these difficulties to the countertransference, Strachey points in this direction:

"at the moment of interpretation the analyst is in fact deliberately evoking a quantity of the patient's id-energy while it is alive and actual and unambiguous and aimed directly at himself. Such a moment must above all others put to the test his relations with his own unconscious impulses" (77). Admittedly, one can shy away from Strachey's particular language. However, what is significant for me is Strachey's sense that the analyst's interpretation emerges from a highly cathected affect directed to the analyst. This must mean that the analyst's responsibility is to clarify her own unconscious contribution, itself a study of the countertransference.

Clarifying one's own contribution in an intersubjective field, however, raises further tensions with situating the countertransference and its uses. Contemporary formulations, as pointed out by Urribarri (2007), bring into the mix the problem of the analytic setting as calling the countertransference, as an "essential dimension of the representational process" (181), and as "being the common cause of the constitution and dynamics of the analytic field" (181). In this view, the countertransference is both a representation and revision of the analytic relationship. It represents what the analytic setting feels like and how these feelings transform the relationship between two unconscious minds. Notably, it is the setting, which composes the analytic relation and its particular frame, that invokes the urge to transform affects into representations. Less noticed is that what also transforms both the analyst and the analysand is their different experiences of not knowing (Kohon 1986b).

If Strachey and Racker give us a clue as to the analyst's feelings and if an intersubjective approach gathers the dispersal of representation, Winnicott's two papers on the countertransference, written twenty years apart, touch upon what breaks the heart of the analytic experience. His first paper has the ominous title "Hate in the Countertransference." Winnicott (1992) makes the important point that "however much [the analyst] loves his patients he cannot avoid hating them and fearing them, and the better he knows this the less will hate and fear be the motives determining what he does to his patients" (195). The paper is mainly about hate as the analyst's response to the emotional burden of the work itself. Winnicott sees in this hate something more than the work of hate and, indeed, argues that unless one can understand the nature of hate, one cannot conceptualize the problem of love. Yet hate, as internalized and externalized, is one of the most powerful forces in life and perhaps one of the most difficult to grasp without repeating what is experienced. I tried to give a glimpse of this earlier when I admitted to my discussion some of my hate in psychoanalytic training. Just as it is difficult for the teacher to understand that her unconscious hatred is there in the classroom, so it is with the analyst to understand that her or his hatred is there in the session. Hatred breaks through the veneer of idealization of the analyst's and teacher's self and the profession's fantasy that the analyst only wants to be a good analyst and the teacher only loves children.

Given the power of the analytic setting to evoke the analyst's countertransference, we may speculate that the classroom works in a similar way, in which case the teacher's countertransference is to education as such. One form this takes is through the teacher's identification with the instituted myths of education. Earlier I referenced the demand in education that the teacher loves children and that this is one of the most powerful myths that lend idealization and confusion to the teacher's function and boundaries. While I believe we may feel surprise when we admit that the teacher hates the children, in Winnicott's view, unless we can make that admission, we neither understand love nor hate. Just as significant, unless the teacher can confront the defenses of idealization and omnipotence in her or his teaching, there will be no real contact with others. Nor will the teacher's countertransference to this myth be recognized.

In my teaching, I give my graduate students this paper by Winnicott and am always surprised at how much they love it. Few of these students see that in giving them this paper, I may be also expressing my hate of them. The problem is that at some level it is difficult to tell the difference between love and hate in learning, specifically because involved in any teaching and learning is a certain ruthlessness, an aggression with both the material taught and with our respective uses of it. The teacher, after all, is a witness to how students ruin her lessons, misinterpret her intentions, refuse to read, hand in late papers, and generally go their own way without thinking about the teacher's plans, schedules, or even her feelings. Students have felt the teacher's ruthlessness in the practice of grading, of writing over their work, and of refusing to accept late papers. Winnicott, however, makes the argument that the analyst's hate—and I shall add to this the teacher's hate—often remain latent: it is there unconsciously and defended against by the ego. We then give ourselves all kinds of reasons for loving our work: we chose it, it is gratifying, we learn things, we like to help, progress gives us rewards, the students/analysands like us, and our parents are proud, for example. Winnicott puts it this way: "[The analyst] cashes in on the success of those who did the dirty work when the patient was an infant" (197). As for the teacher's bankroll, each year the teacher cashes in on all that came before the school year begins. And when the teacher cannot cash in, so to say, the bankrupt teacher of the previous year is blamed.

Our good reasons for doing the work, many of which are idealizing however, do not take away the analyst or the teacher's anxieties, frustrations, and irritations. Idealization does not help the analyst or teacher understand how the demands of the work affect the self who is working. Nor can idealization indicate itself as a defense against loss, or the loneliness that threads its way through the work. When Winnicott wrote of the hate in the countertransference he located one of its sources: "the analyst must be prepared to bear strain without expecting the patient to know anything about what he is doing, perhaps over a long period of time. To do this, he must be easily aware of his own fear and hate" (198). Winnicott believes that the analyst's position is not so different from the mother's relation to the infant. And he speculates that the mother hates the baby before the baby hates the mother. The rest of his paper gives us nineteen or so experiences of the mother's hate. When I ask my students to read this article by Winnicott, we play with these reasons by substituting the teacher's hate of the student. Surely one can also put the student's hate of the teacher there as well, but the purpose is to consider how the teacher experiences ordinary events in extraordinary ways. Here are a few of Winnicott's statements:

The baby is not her own (mental) conception.

The baby is not magically produced.

At first he does not know at all what she does or what she sacrifices for him. Especially he cannot allow for her hate.

He is ruthless, treats her as scum, an unpaid servant, a slave.

He is suspicious, refuses her good food, and makes her doubt herself, but eats well with his aunt.

He excites her but frustrates—she mustn't eat him or trade in sex with him. (201)

Noting these ordinary experiences are not made to congratulate the mother on her sacrifices and her altruism. Instead, they touch upon the mother's boundary that the baby creates for the mother and the differences between them. These experiences frustrate and disillusion the mother's omnipotence and narcissism, which the baby is allowed to do and indeed, needs the mother to experience for a self to develop. And because the mother was once a baby who leaned on this allowance, what remains of these omnipotent feelings and their history of disillusionment and loss returns to the mother with great force. The couple reminds the mother of her hate. This last turn of Winnicott's paper is perhaps the most difficult to accept. While the mother must hate the baby without acting it out, her hate may be conveyed only through putting the baby to bed, lending the baby the terror of nursery rhymes and fairy tales of children being eaten or lost in the woods, and, eventually, sending the baby to school. But the baby, too, needs this hate because the baby "needs hate to hate" (202) and also because the baby needs to know that it affects mother. That is, in order to develop her own complexities and desires, the baby needs—as do our students and colleagues—to encounter a passionate, complex other.

Many years later Winnicott (1988) wrote a second paper, "Countertransference," noting that his first paper was really about hate while the new paper was meant as a communication to the psychoanalytic field. His message was that the term *countertransference* had become so overstretched in psychoanalytic debate, so ready at hand to describe any feeling the analyst had at any time, that it was in danger of losing its technical focus. I have the sense that Winnicott was losing patience with his colleagues, fatigued by the old argument of whether the analyst's own analysis was at stake in the interpretation of the countertransference. The paper reminds analysts about a different limit to the work itself. He seemed to suggest that not everything was countertransference. He told his audience: "Professional work is quite different from ordinary life, is it not?" (263). One difference is that there are specific strains in the work in maintaining a professional attitude: "A professional attitude may, of course, be built up on a basis of defenses and inhibitions and obssesional orderliness, and I suggest that it is here that the psychotherapist is particularly under strain, because any structuring of his ego-defenses lessens his ability to meet the new situation" (264). Another novelty is with the analyst's function and her commitment to the analytic frame, which is also different from ordinary life. Yet the working professional must remain vulnerable because she works with her own mind. For Winnicott, this means that the analyst's countertransference is not just any response but one that indicates and represents the idea that the line between professional work and ordinary life has been lost.

Winnicott's understanding of countertransference seems to be a variation on Freud's view with the proviso that the focus is on the work itself: "Insofar as all this is true," Winnicott writes, "the meaning of the word countertransference can only be the neurotic features that spoil the professional attitude and disturb the course of the analytic process as determined by the patient" (266). In other words, the experience of countertransference is to be used as a way to conceptualize the fragility of the professional's boundaries between self and other and as a commentary on the limits of the work itself. In my view, this last paper raises a significant paradox in the impossible professions.

The miasma of ordinary life is always threatening to dissolve the artifice of psychoanalysis and professional life lends an added burden to the professional. For if we must lean upon our emotional life and our defenses against feeling helpless or misused or misunderstood in our work with others in order to conceptualize the emotional world of the other and our uncertainty, and if our work contributes to that life that then contributes to our capacity to work, given emotional life's fluidity and its tendencies to forget its permutations and boundaries, the countertransference presents us with this remainder, itself an unconscious communication on the difficulties of separation and difference.

"TAILPIECE"

When friends learn that I am training to become a psychoanalyst and that I am in private practice, they first ask, "How do you do it?" The question is familiar; teachers are asked the same one. But the "it" referred to takes us into what is unspeakable about the history of our learning, about times when one did go crazy or felt as if one would just break apart. My friends seem to be asking about so many experiences, beginning with what they imagine goes on in my consulting room, perhaps with a worry that they are undergoing a secret psychoanalysis each time we speak. Are boundaries being broken? They may wish for me to listen to their complaints, anxieties, hatred, and stories of disappointments. Then they may wonder why anyone would want to do such work. Beyond these problems of separating who is doing what to whom, some imagine that my training in psychoanalysis prepares me for "it" and so I never have to ask myself, how *do* I do it? And yet, like learning to teach, there is no way to prepare for the uncertainties and emotional demands of the practice; there is no protection from the vulnerability, doubts, fears, and bouts of helplessness made when one tries to understand another as one tries to understand the self. There is no agreement as to what it means to not understand, to encounter the work's limits, the limited self, the hurt feelings, and still continue working. And there is no way to prepare for the surprise of the forceful countertransference.

One of my teachers, a senior analyst, used to joke when asked how he does the work day after day. He said "All I do is show up." This analyst did not explain much more, but I found myself thinking a great deal about what it can mean to show up, what it means to offer one's emotional presence without knowing in advance what else can happen. When the analyst (and, we should add, the teacher) shows up each day, she proves to the analysand (and student) that anxieties have not destroyed the analyst, that grudges belong to ordinary life, that speaking about them is not the same as carrying them out even if it feels like it, and that, in the analytic setting, inviting ordinary life in the form of speech brings to the setting what is extraordinary and most abstract about it. The same rule applies to the analysand. By showing up each day, she shows the analyst that the analyst's mistakes did not kill off the work, that there is something about the violence of interpretation that can be accepted, and that together, even with old material, they can write a new page.

As a way into the uncertainty of the work in terms of its difficult boundaries and our limitations, the question, how do you do it, can also be taken through what Winnicott (2001) spoke of as the paradox of "the conception-perception gap" (151). Winnicott proposes that conception, or the theory of and anticipation for experience, comes before perception. Perception has to do with what one finds in experience, which differs from what one anticipates. It comes afterward. But this means that the object affects theory, signifying the gap between them. Winnicott urges us to see this gap as a needed place of study and as uncloseable. It makes me think that education as well lives in this gap and creates the gap in which it lives.

My friends also find it funny to see me back in school. They know me enough to know that I was one of those children who grew up hating it and who has difficulty following directions. I suppose my revenge was to become a professor. Now, with my analytic training, I continue seeking this revenge for having to learn by attempting to understand my experience as a candidate through the countertransference, itself a dialogue with my own history of object relation learning. If trying to understand my countertransference gives me access to how my learning is made from deep regressions, defenses, and phantasies of education, there is a great deal to learn about these theories and how one's education may welcome this work that is already occurring. The surprise of the teacher's countertransference is that she refinds her own student self as countertransference with education. I show up in my education with all of these affects, but am beginning to understand that these feelings of love and hate, my countertransference to education, need not end in a showdown, for, after all, education is different from ordinary life, even if it draws from what is most unresolved there. Indeed, the gap between conception and perception is education's playground. But this raises the question of whether the very structure and thought of this education can tolerate how our love and hate plays there.

CHAPTER SIX

TRANSFERENCE PEOPLE

O, fair,
O, strange voice,
it is right
that you ask
why I weep;
I looked on this house,
I was caught
by an ancient regret

—From Kreousa's lament in
H.D.'s (2003) adaptation of *Ion*

AESTHETIC CONFLICTS

In 1933, the poet H.D., then forty-seven years old, traveled from London to Vienna for psychoanalysis with the seventy-seven-year-old Freud. The analysis, conducted in English, was to last three months.[1] They met five times a week and, when not in analysis, H.D. wrote letters, read, went to the cinema and opera, and joined artists, poets, writers, actors, and the friends in her circle. A decade later, H.D. (1974) began writing her eloquent, dream-like construction of the analysis. In these pages, she remembers her first words and then Freud's reply as she began the session with her desire to find the root of her distress. Only retrospectively could she understand how she held her habitual past tightly as Freud drew her to their unknown present. Between bouts of weeping, she may have told Freud and now us readers: "I would deliberately assemble all the sorry memories in my effort to get at the truth. He said, 'We never know what is important or what is unimportant until after.' He said, 'We must be impartial, see fair play to ourselves'" (119).

Perhaps Freud touched upon questions she already had. How does one recount a life without falling back on deadening habits? From where does the truth of one's life emerge? And, if H.D. is to be an artist in the world, in a world of war, intolerance, and violence, what kind of artist can she be?

Freud's invitation was ironic: narrate all that inhibits your words. Or, perhaps, put into speech all that is not speech. He said, "We never know what is important or what is unimportant until after" (119). Today, we may understand this psychoanalytic impartiality as urging an aesthetic distance from repeating our "sorry memories" and as a clearing for new understanding of events that could not have been understood at the time of their unfolding. Artists, too, cultivate aesthetic distance, even discordance, between the raw events that become experience and its afterlife in symbolization; they make from the ruins of what feels utterly wrecked a new beginning. The dynamic of imagination—what we in education may also call the labor of thinking—represents these fissures of then and now. Imagination places the heart of learning to live within the problems we have with tendentious meaning. Let us try to see this work of imagination as a response to understanding our responsibility.

This chapter presents a few artists from the vantage of their efforts to express the inexpressible in history—their personal history and the history to which they responded. But rather than simply narrate some interesting stories and leave these artists confined to their historical dramas, I place our present concern—what education can mean as a practice of imagination—into tension with the historicity of these artists' lives and comment on our responsibility toward what these artists have left us. The history they lived becomes for us an encounter with our own time of testimony. Freud (1914a) named such efforts with the past "working through," when the persistent encounter with the traumatic past—what resists time and words—can become narrated as a problem for memory and testimony. We will meet again H.D. and other artists and writers such as Rilke, Mahler, and Walter. Some sought or called upon psychoanalysis to understand the great problem of what in the world— the internal and the external world—inhibits words and thus the imagination. They will be presented not through their accomplishments, although I celebrate their work, but from the side of their doubts, inhibitions, aesthetic conflicts, and then how they understood the failure of imagination and its reparation. Psychoanalysis as well will be presented from the vantage of its doubts, its uncertainties, and its reparative use of the arts. We will see efforts to understand unconscious life, where things are never what they appear to be, where the accidents of life become fused with a story of desire, destruction, and history, and where the repressed carries both the symptoms of violence and its fears of representation.

I call the figures in this chapter "transference people"[2] because they provide me with an opportunity to explore our internal world as composed from the libidinal relations we lend to and take in from others, and that create the erotic ties we need for symbolization. Certainly, my approach takes seriously the freedom of imagination, following along the lines of how Kristeva (1998) postulated freedom as "synonymous with an interiority to be created in relation to an external world to be internalized . . . freedom as the internalization of the outside, if and only if this outside (to begin with, the mother) allows for play and lets itself be played with" (11). While not speaking specifically about the formation of the ego, Kristeva's sense of freedom is intimate. Her concern is with the transference or the creation of the ego as that aesthetic link made from internalizing and externalizing the world of others. My "transference people" permit play with the idea that there is a double difficulty in conceptualizing the poetics and promise of the imagination: all at once we are reminded of our dependency to others and to the unknown world. Imagination is dependent on what is enigmatic in psychical life *and* a response to the unknown outside world. More concretely, through artists' encounters with psychoanalysis and in psychoanalytic encounters with the arts we glimpse a new orientation for understanding imagination, as a counterdepressive force against intolerance. Understanding imagination is both an enigmatic resource and responsibility for education. After all, when the field of education encounters the failure of imagination, it confronts both its own crisis of responsibility and its relation to others. We face the same choice Freud presented to H.D. We can stay on the side of the failure of imagination and its repetitive grammar by insisting that we know in advance what is important and unimportant or we can try again to encounter the unknown.

H.D.'s analysis, which I'll return to shortly, began with an aesthetic conflict—what Meltzer and Williams(1988) defines as a confrontation with "the enigmatic quality of the object" (27). The object is available to the senses, yet invokes doubts and mental pain over the nature of understanding the inner world as an already internalized relation to the absent other. Appreciation of what is ineffable about self and other relations is, for Meltzer and Williams, a question for the imagination. And the large question is whether imagination can contain the agony of "the tragic element in the aesthetic experience" (27). Because the aesthetic conflict entangles doubt with loss and beauty with destruction, imagination—or the capacity to bring what is absent into symbols—must work overtime to grasp where it can fail. Now what is interesting to consider is that Meltzer and Williams place our first aesthetic conflict within natality and so within the human condition of having to be born into helplessness and dependency and be met this way by the unknown world of others. They imagine the infant is called into life by the mother's beauty, then mesmerized by her mysteries, then anxious over her loss. The creating of this relational bond excites the infant's desire for her or his own mind and, too, the anxieties and phantasies that make this mind an area of conflict, knowledge, and desire.

There are two intimate enigmatic object worlds: the inner world of drives, phantasies, and object relations and the external world of others, culture, and historical reality. This is what I think Kristeva (1998) meant when she saw interiority as created "in relation to an external world to be internalized" (11) and when she proposed this freedom as vulnerable to the other's capacity for play. For Meltzer and Williams, too, the inner world of object relations is made from being with others, the condition for our desire that leads them to claim: "Desire makes it possible, even essential to give the object its freedom" (27). What belongs solely to the subject, what the subject becomes responsive to and eventually carries a responsibility toward, is the conflict between her or his drive to possess the other to center the self and her or his desire to choose freedom, even if this choice is also a source of pain. Thus, their claim that without aesthetic conflicts, without internal doubts and anxieties over the loss of the other, there can be no imagination for the external world. The supposition is that both psychical reality and material reality are enigmatic, not just subject to the unknown but part of the unknown. Together, these inner and outer realms must be symbolized over and over. And this symbolization will constitute memory and freedom from it. The supposition is that we begin within conflicts of love and hate and with a preoccupation with beauty and its loss. And with this formulation, which places aesthetic conflict at the heart of affinity and loss, psychoanalysis becomes a poetics of subjectivity, designating narrative as its expressive art.

Perhaps one of the most courageous questions we can ask ourselves is this: from where does one find the artistic truth of one's life? This was certainly a question for H.D. Freud implied that artistic or emotional truth is made only within the play of impartiality. While Kristeva reminds us that fair play is the responsibility of that first other, Meltzer and Williams consider the new and tragic element of responsibility that is yet to be made from giving the object its freedom. This courage to play within the unknown, I think, is the necessary gamble for imagination. Yet in times of social strife, there is pressure to be loyal to a one-sided reality; there is pressure to comply and to give up one's own mind. Recall that H.D.'s analysis occurs in Vienna in the growing shadow of Nazi Germany. By 1933, impartiality, or the capacity to listen, to speak freely, to choose an uncensored artistic life was under attack. It was the year Hitler became the German chancellor in Berlin and the year of book burnings there—Freud's as well as others.[3] There, too, the Third Reich would deem music by Jewish composers as *Entartete Musik* or "degenerate music."[4] Today, we can listen to this banned music, pondering its censorship and its beauty. Today, the city of Berlin holds a library reading week to commemorate the book burnings of 1933. We can think of the censorship of the arts in our own time of war. We can wonder how the arts come to be deemed offensive and consider what else is lost when freedom of imagination is feared.

In 1933, after his concerts were banned by the Nazis, the conductor Bruno Walter, whom you will meet shortly, fled Berlin for Vienna (Ryding and Pechefsky 2001).[5] That year, too, writing from Berlin, novelist Joseph Roth (2003) would, in anguish, report of the books being burned and the artists under attack. And he would proclaim the artists' defeat by their own society and their own capitulations when he wrote: "The European mind is capitulating. It is capitulating out of weakness, out of sloth, out of apathy, out of lack of imagination (it will be the task of some future generation to establish the reasons for this disgraceful capitulation)" (207). The attack on artists, he implied, was no different from destroying anyone's mind. Today, we may consider that an attack on the arts is an attack on impartiality, itself the condition for creative work that lends imagination its freedom.

Sixty years later, with a quiet monument, Humboldt University in Berlin now commemorates that place where the books were burned. In the Bebelplatz, across from the Law School, one finds "The Empty Library" created in 1995 by the Israeli artist Micha Ullman. This underground monument is easy to miss and walk over. But there is a small glass pane embedded in the cobble walkway, its surface scratched by weather and the scuff marks of shoes. One must crouch low to see what lies below. Then, one encounters only empty bookcases lining its four walls to mark our memory with this erasure and loss. A small plaque, also on the ground, quotes the poet Heinrich Heine, who wrote a century before: "Where they start by burning books, they'll end by burning people."

So, too, in the newly built Jewish Museum of Berlin, the contributions and loss of German Jewry are memorialized. It is not supposed to be a Holocaust museum, yet its jagged architecture and its narrative of destruction lead the viewer to what is most unthinkable about the Shoah. Indeed, near the exit sits a small television screen. It was there that I watched the endless loop of a 1964 edited interview with Hannah Arendt, which took place in what does not exist anymore, West Germany. I became mesmerized by what I thought was Arendt's insistence that it was not the year of 1933 that so affected her generation. Instead, with the terrible hindsight of living after, she said, it was when they heard of Auschwitz. When the interviewer asked why, she replied, or I thought she replied, "The bodies." This, for her, she said, was the abyss, what should never have happened but in fact did happen.

Then and now psychoanalysis resides within this paradox of tying the threads of imagination to brute reality: even as words became an enemy to destroy, it would be only words that would repair the soul and narrate the societal depression. The words used to destroy the mind and our capacity to think—by 1933, it was Nazi law, censorship, street violence, and propaganda; today we may ponder our own wars—would have to be met with other words to lend to the loss of the mind the significance needed for its repair. H.D.'s analysis, too, resided in this paradox. As books were being burned and as H.D. found it difficult to write, psychoanalysis would only propose, to lend relief to her depression, the free association with words. In the memoir of her analysis written ten years later, still in the midst of war, H.D.'s reconstruction extends Freud's first advice. She permitted the important and the unimportant to have their say and even affect what is tragic for both. In this literary affair, in the affair that is psychoanalysis, we are requested to suspend preconceptions, themselves a defense against the unknown. And H.D.'s memoir plays with this advice. In her tribute to Freud, she wrote of walking in the streets of Vienna where "tiny confetti-like tokens" (58) fell to the ground. H.D. reported their message: "Hitler gives bread, Hitler gives work" (58). Her testimony many years later carries her own reply: it reads as if she tore her memories into a thousand tiny pieces, threw them above her head, and then, like so much confetti, witnessed their drift, how her memories, no longer fixated in the timelessness of the unconscious, could now scatter into something new.

H.D. AND FREUD

Before that aesthetic achievement, which for H.D. had to be won over and over, there was the difficult beginning of analysis: her first impressions and the aesthetic conflicts they conveyed. In her daily letters written to others during 1933 and 1934 and in the later memoir of the analysis, we learn that the beauty of Freud's consulting room first overwhelmed H.D. She (1974) would later recall that Freud handed her his favorite statue, Pallas Athené: "'She's perfect' he said, *only she has lost her spear*'. I didn't say anything" (69). Then again, H.D. returned to how this felt to her: "She had lost her spear. He might have been talking Greek . . . although he was speaking English without a perceptible trace of accent, yet he was speaking a foreign language" (69).

On that first day of her analysis with Freud, she could not stop looking at Freud's collection of objects of antiquity, the couch draped with an Oriental rug and then the chair placed behind it, the books he would sometimes lend her later, and the desk that held, perhaps, his favorite ancient artifacts lined up in such a way that, when sitting behind his desk, Freud might hide, take refuge in the play of his own writing. H.D. felt the consulting room as museum of tiny treasures for her to discover: here the preserved past was still affecting its own mysteries and now, through the transference, she, too, would affect and rewrite her mythology. And the room itself seemed to invite her private mythology, with the proviso that it be interpreted as always under construction, subject to play, and also to loss and to mourning. H.D. would learn it is not that the events of her life, what she first called her "sorry memories," that would themselves change. But her understanding of memory's work would. What became the core of the analysis was the work of understanding the failure of imagination, so devastating for the writer and, ultimately, for the social imaginary in which writers live.

Freud's accidental pedagogy, if I could put it this way, began with bits of advice. He was telling the writer not to prepare a draft of each session prior to their meeting, that the material would emerge without her effort to control what should be said or how her words would be heard, and that together in free association, they would create the courage needed to meet the unknown. Ever the writer, even when in the throes of her writing block—of needing to say something but having no words—H.D. wished her memories to have, for him, drama and narrative flair. It was, after all, what she hoped for her own art but it was also where she felt most dissatisfied. Freud was not interested in this performance; he needed only her rough, unprepared drafts. H.D. (1974) writes of needed negations: "He said again that he did not want me to prepare. I could not explain adequately that I did not. He does not, apparently, want me to take notes, but I must do that" (165). And indeed, "the Professor" as she sometimes called Freud in the memoir and "papa," which she called him in the letters, continued to ask her, when the material flattened her curiosity, if she has prepared for the analysis.

One preparation, having to do with the work of the unconscious, was permitted. H.D. could not stop preparing in the form of magnificent dreams she made for Freud. And it surprised her when Freud asked for her interpretations, when he found delight in her play. Yet when pressed for details, she hardly remembered the historical facts, or else, when the forgotten details suddenly came into view and so became the *camera obscura*, they presented some other story than the one she may have desired. Let this negativity emerge, Freud seemed to say, as he invited her to narrate her phantasies of history and associate freely with what she herself had made from the accidents of her life, from lost chances and loss of love, from what she could not make happen, and from what she could not explain but nonetheless felt. Her responsibility would be a commitment to symbolize this unknown. After the analysis, I think, H.D. began to learn why history is so difficult for the psyche, how this difficulty impresses and obscures memory, and why the work of becoming responsive to the unknown matters for living an artistic life.

As I read through her letters and memoir, I wondered whether H.D. had difficulty tolerating her otherness—as modernist poet, as woman, as bisexual—and so suffered from a particular failure of imagination. She suggests as much in her memoir of the analysis, but refuses to secure the source of her distress in the social disparagement of her plurality. After all, H.D. felt isolation but was not isolated. She was a part of a larger, lively expressive revolt committed only to the imagination. Today, we might understand her circle as "Queer" in that she and her friends embraced the artists' diasporas, crossing racial, ethnic, sexual, geographic, and imaginary boundaries. They had their neurosis, but also took great pleasure in the know-how of their transgressions. They protested inequalities in the world and enjoyed how their art defied conventionality to break open the repressed of symbolization. So I think the otherness that agonized H.D. was of a different order than the one we typically associate with the pains of social difference. What held her back, what was particular about her anguish, cannot be placed neatly into a personal response to social disregard. Nor would her anguish be extinguished solely through recognition, although this would help. Perhaps we are touching upon the tragic aspect of life when we raise the question of what is enigmatic about the unconscious and its otherness. Here then is our original relation to the unknowable. And while psychoanalysis may sometimes render this intimacy as agony and even invite anguish and sadness by way of interpretation, this aesthetic conflict is given free play.

Freud told her not to prepare and gave her two other instructions: first, that she was not to discuss her analysis with anyone and, second, she was never to defend him. We know from her letters and memoir that H.D. broke both rules; she kept a journal of their 1933 sessions and wrote daily letters about her analysis to her intimate patron and friend Bryher and to others as well (Friedman 2002). The memoir came later, not as defense but as gratitude and reparation. Freud, too, broke his own rules. His archive of letters is filled with psychoanalytic misadventures, bad advice, the failures of defense, and the anguish of his own self-analysis. Almost all of his published writing constitutes a defense of psychoanalysis, for he understood the anxiety, fear, uncertainty, and hatred his method invoked. Nor did he shy away from his own doubts. Sometimes charming and at other times deflating, Freud's writing carries a double voice, addressed to believers and disbelievers, to impartial people and to those enraged. He anticipated and even welcomed the resistance to his method. And throughout his career he continued to write for the general public, lecture to civic groups, and pressure his theories with the expression of artists, his own doubts, and his aesthetic conflicts. But also, in the case of this daily analysis with H.D., his impartiality was always threatened by the transference between them: gifts were exchanged; there was shared gossip, and some contact beyond the analysis. And the transference obeyed neither reality nor psychoanalytic convention. As with all transference, it became both an obstacle to the analysis and its needed resource for the work, only to be eventually sublimated.

When Freud requested that H.D. never defend him, he was well aware that others could see psychoanalysis as indicating not just a personal failure, oversusceptibility to its method, or as a waste of one's time. It could be also thought of as a betrayal of friendship. H.D.'s letters suggest as much and her friendship with Ezra Pound, for example, suffered when he accused her of choosing Freud over him. Yet the primary reason for not becoming Freud's defender turns on the psychoanalytic problem of resistance, which is itself a theory of learning. Defending psychoanalysis would only make the one who dismisses it angry. Rationality neither cures intolerance nor revives the failure of the imagination. And let us admit that one can hardly be rational in the face of intolerance. Surely clinical work helped Freud understand the affective difficulty of changing one's mind, the need to have both hated and beloved objects, the terror and paranoia made when one feels love is being taken away, and the sorrow, indeed, the mourning, that accompanies disillusionment. Her *Tribute to Freud* rehearses what she remembered of his reasons, now seeming to address the reader:

> You will do no good to the detractor by mistakenly beginning a logical
> defense. You will drive the hatred or the fear or the prejudice deeper. You
> will do no good to yourself, for you will only expose your own feelings. . . .
> You will do no good to me and my work, for antagonism, once taking
> hold, cannot be rooted out from above the surface, and it thrives, in a way,
> on heated argument and digs in deeper. The only way to extract the fear
> or prejudice would be from within, from below, and as naturally this type
> of prejudiced or frightened mind would dodge any hint of a suggestion of
> psychoanalytic treatment, or even, put it, study and research along these
> lines, you cannot get to the root of the trouble. Every word, spoken in my
> defense, I mean, to already prejudiced individuals, serves to drive the root
> in deeper. (86–87)

Yet words were all that could be traded in the consulting room, and as Adam
Phillips (2006) has suggested in his introduction to the new literary translations of Freud, "Freud is the writer for people who want to find out what
words may have done to them, and may still be doing" (vii). Words, however,
as Freud warned H.D., get under one's skin even if there is also a denial that
words can really matter.

For this very reason—that putting things into words matter to the
writer—Freud desired analysands who were artists. In his book of mistakes
Freud (1901) said as much: "In the field of symptomatic acts, too, psychoanalytic observation must concede priority to imaginative writers" (17).
Already they knew the power of words as capable of clearing confusion and
expressing its affects. Already they presented our emotional world as subject
to what could not be seen or experienced and gave a story to unconscious
conflicts that animate our relations to others. Already they presented what
is disagreeable in reality and in doing so show us how reality is susceptible
to that which is not reality at all. Already they depict the terror that ensues
when meaning breaks down, when hatred overtakes the mind, when the
imagination fails, when motives cut lose from their purpose, and when one
devises an inhibition or meets with despair a prohibition against thought.
Already they put into speech all that is not speech. And they affect us with
their affect, creating for our mind, new transference people, new aesthetic
conflicts that invite us to play.

Freud's relation to the arts, however, was both a source of inspiration and
an index of his own ambivalence in trying to understand the mythology of
the mind (Britzman 2006). He was always interested in creativity and while
he had so many theories as to what stops it short—what inhibits desire and
what collapses meaning into stultifying routine—he could never quite answer

the question: where does creativity come from? In his essay on the creative writer and daydreaming, Freud (1908) wondered: "from what sources that strange being, the creative writer, draws his material, and how he manages to make such an impression on us with it and to arouse in us emotions of which, perhaps, we had not even thought ourselves capable" (143). The best Freud could do was to suggest the creativity of imagination as a paradox: the creative writer works with the products of phantasy without the defense of reality, yet does not turn away from reality or phantasy. Artists may lend insight into the terrible confusion of these two realms and in so doing posit memory itself as a question. They present an uncanny index of the doubts that rush in and the terrible cost of not distinguishing one's projections from the enigmatic object. Indeed, the paradox is that the arts can symbolize the social and individual failure of imagination; they can present our passion for ignorance without recourse to defending reality. Perhaps it was from imaginative works that Freud made sense of the creative power of impartiality and the patience to play with the nonsense of the unconscious.

H.D. sought analysis with Freud because she suffered from a writing inhibition. She could not finish manuscripts, hated the work she had done, and felt stagnant in her creativity. She felt like a man when she wrote and a woman when she didn't and this terrible split was paralyzing. Why her distress migrated to matters of gender was part of the analysis, although, to my mind, putting this conflict into words presented H.D., and now us, with new questions: how are our bodies lived as phantasy, as contradiction, and as wish and desire? What is it to play with misrecognition and lost others? There were, of course, unspoken desires and bisexual yearnings somehow entangled in her distress over the impending war that returned with great anguish the traumatic losses she experienced in World War I. Yet how brave she must have been to travel to Vienna in 1933 to meet with an ailing Freud who was already beginning to experience the persecution that would lead in 1938 to his exile.

H.D. wrote of one regret in her memoir: that she never asked Freud how he felt about the growing anti-Semitism of Vienna. Both of them were aware of that present danger, but what it would come to mean could not yet be known. They often spoke about the street violence and the beatings of Jews by Nazi gangs. Yet in a letter she wrote to Bryher on March 22, 1933, during her analysis, she does know how Freud feels. She writes Bryher with worries over Freud's safety and recounts how she tries to reassure him that the worst will not happen, that the world will not let the worst happen. Freud was unconvinced, she reported to Bryher, and then reminded her of what is important now: "He says, '. . . many, many, people will be murdered.' (He meant Jews.) I said I didn't think massacre was possible, there was still the open sympathy of the world. Poor old, old little old papa. However, he gave a flea-shake to his shoulders and said, 'well, we better go on with your analysis. It's the only thing now.' So, on we plunged" (Friedman 2002, p. 135).

Two months later, H.D. left Vienna suddenly after a bomb scare on the streetcar. She returned again in 1934 for another two months of analysis with Freud. Again, more rules were broken and they continued to face war. When she left Freud again, she carried with her the old problem of trying to write. The cure would take longer than the analysis, but a seed of cure had already been planted by Freud's insistence that even in times of war and its destruction, even when individuals are the last beings to matter, even when understanding one's emotional life has only the power to affect the self, her analysis did matter as did her struggle to live, against all odds, an artistic life.

OTHER ARTISTS: RILKE, MAHLER, AND WALTER

H.D. was not the only artist Freud analyzed but she may have been his last and, to my mind, the most eloquent poet of psychoanalysis. We now meet a few other artists who encountered Freud, beginning with the poet Rilke in 1915, then back to the composer Mahler in 1910, and then further back to Mahler's protégé, the conductor Bruno Walter in 1906. Like H.D., each artist suffered from his own crisis of creativity, made from that potent and singular combination of life's accidents, personal failings, loss of love, worries over success and failure, and the fraying of libidinal ties in an uncertain world. They all felt conflicted over what, in living an artistic life, is important and unimportant. And with each encounter we meet an affected Freud interested in both destruction and creativity, in beauty and violence, and so with accepting the sudden expression and the slow symbolization of aesthetic conflicts.

The poet Rilke met Freud during World War I. Today, we may consider him as the negative of H.D. in that he did not want an analysis. Subject to depressive bouts and doubts over his creativity, Rilke never quite made it into Freud's consulting room. The analyst Lou Andre Salome, Freud's colleague and Rilke's great friend, did her best to suggest that he see Freud (von Unwerth 2005). Rilke did visit the Freuds socially in 1915 and while Freud invited him back, he never returned. Like so many artists and intellectuals, Rilke felt that his madness—his depression and his oddities—were necessary to his creative life's work. Perhaps he is half right, for we do need our private madness to even approach the question of imagination. Where he went wrong, in my view, is with what he imagined psychoanalysis would do to him. He worried that psychoanalysis would erase his creative edge, make him normal, and so cure him from writing at all. Rilke felt his neurosis as a needed treasure, even if it also carried his mental pain. But he must have also questioned, during depressive bouts of sadness and despair, when he could find neither words nor beauty, whether his writing was a symptom of the illness or its inspiration. This aesthetic conflict is one Kristeva (1989) claims for the literary struggle, that "literary creation . . . constitute[s] a very faithful semiological representation of the subject's battle with symbolic collapse" (24). And if Rilke's poetry is a testament to this struggle, so, too, is psychoanalysis.

Freud never formally mentioned his fleeting relation with Rilke, but in the beautiful imaginative history of their meeting, von Unwerth (2005) places the haunted figure of Rilke into the center of Freud's (1916) poignant paper, "On Transience," which was written during World War I. There, Freud muses over a walk in the woods, taken with a young friend and with another person he called "a young but already famous poet" (305). Perhaps it was the poet Rilke. This poet was joyless, overcome by his doubts on the fleeting life of nature's beauty. Why, he asked, should I care about the beauty of nature if all living things must die? And why would one love if loss was the inevitable ending? Wouldn't it be better not to love? These grand questions and their painful plaint Freud considered as a symptom of mourning the illness of the human condition. The only consolation Freud could think of was that beauty's impermanence, its transience, lends beauty its value, gifts, and our gratitude. But the impermanence also touches our doubts over loss and thoughts of death. Beauty calls forth our aesthetic conflicts and so fleeting beauty will be inevitably linked to mortality and its loss. It was in this paper Freud first proposed that the capacity to appreciate beauty is affected through the work of mourning even as this work must include attaching memory to loss and finding again a new and different world with the living.

Freud took another walk in 1910, this time with a composer of music. Like the poets H.D. and Rilke, Mahler, too, broke open conventional form to imagine lost worlds that never existed and, in the same gesture, bid them welcome and farewell. He tormented the height of romanticism with the negativity of its destruction; sounds of the new clashed against the old, conflicts of illusion and disillusion made revelation. There played in his music the untimely time of the aesthetic conflicts. Freud was fifty-four years old when he walked with the fifty-year-old Gustav Mahler. The consultation lasted four hours, and occurred just a year before Mahler's death. Stuart Feder (2004) tenderly recreates their brief encounter, what he imagines as "the walking cure" (206), suggesting that, by the time of the consultation, Mahler's creative capacity to integrate emotional crisis into his music had foundered.

Adorno's (1992) study of Mahler's music also alludes to his consultation with Freud. There Mahler's music is likened to Freud's early cathartic method, where the psychodrama of affects, so fixated on traumatic events, are revived for memory to loosen the past's hold on the present. What strikes Adorno, perhaps a shadow of Rilke's fear, is that Freud "declined to cure his person out of respect for his work" (39). We might consider that Freud approached anyone this way since for him cure only meant the capacity to work and love. Still, Adorno rails against any suggestion that a psychological analysis of Mahler' crisis does any justice to his creative work. There is, for Adorno, an objective reality beyond psychology. Yet the psychology remains when Adorno wrote, "Mahler's music is the individual's dream of the irresistible collective. But at the same time it expresses objectively the impossibility of identification with it" (33). Music, he implies, composes history as a crisis with its own dreams. Music, he implies, begins with our aesthetic conflict of beauty and loss.

I suppose Freud's brief encounters with Rilke and Mahler point to the difficulty of understanding together creative life with the artists' despair over its loss. I imagine these walks with the poet and the composer leave us with new questions as to the nature of creative life, its relation to the artists' time, and what within the artist stops it short. We can wonder, for instance, about external conditions as the obstacle to understanding its own imaginary but that would leave out our freedom, how we internalize the world of others and express this world. Their work, after all, leaves behind a story of beauty and destruction; we receive the symbolization of desires from their vanishing point: what has not lasted or even what could have never existed. Theirs was a faith that symbolization, as the attempt to encounter what is absent, mattered. Expressions of this play, including the moment it can shatter, take us to the realm of what is most difficult in imagining living in our world. The analysis of Mahler's associate, the conductor Bruno Walter, allows us a closer look into the idiomatic details of this struggle and the relation between aesthetic conflict and sudden responsibility.

Walter began his analysis with Freud in 1906. Psychoanalysis was a new theory and treatment, but it already suffered from an illicit reputation due to Freud's exploration of infantile sexuality and his insistence on the vicissitudes of Eros. Walter consulted Freud because he had developed an arm paralysis, a catastrophic symptom for an orchestral conductor and surely a crisis of creativity and confidence. No physical cause could be ascertained and Walter was afraid that he would no longer be able to conduct. Years later in his slim volume on music, Walter (1961) would write that the conductor "guides and influences the playing of others" (83). The responsibility is terrible and terrifying: "The moral danger which, at the same time, is an artistic one, lies for the conductor in the power he has over others" (121). Still, the conductor, alone, is responsible for his ear and hand. And here is where the crisis erupts: the hand loses its assurance, marches of doubts overwhelm the mind, and one's inner sense of the music is lost. In his volume on music, Walter tells us that in this crisis, the conductor's overreliance on technique will only provoke more difficulties.

Sixty years after he saw Freud, Walter (1966) writes in his memoir: "The consultation took a course I had not foreseen. Instead of questioning me about sexual aberrations in infancy, as my layman's ignorance had led me to expect, Freud examined my arm briefly" (164). Then Freud asked him if he had ever traveled to Sicily, told Walter to travel there that night, forget about his arm and use his eyes. This he did and while the vacation relaxed Walter, his arm was not cured. On his next visit, Freud told Walter to continue conducting. Here is how Walter (1966) recalls their conversation: ""But I can't move my arm." "Try it, at any rate," "And what if I should have to stop?" "You won't have to stop." "Can I take upon myself the responsibility of possibly upsetting a performance?" "I'll take responsibility"" (167).

Freud's cure was not miraculous and, in another report of their encounter, Walter is suspicious as to whether his analysis did in fact help (Ryding and Pechefsky 2001). But what is most striking to me about Walter's memoir is his gratitude toward Freud's willingness to relieve him of a responsibility further burdened by his anxiety of not being able to work. What, after all, could Freud actually do when Walter stood to face the orchestra? How could he ever take responsibility for Walter's failure to conduct? And yet I think Freud's willingness to be used and maybe even blamed, his willingness to become one of Walter's transference people, should something bad happen, may have opened Walter to a different understanding of his anxieties; that while he felt such danger, he was not alone. Indeed, the analysis did allow Walter to reconsider and change many of his ideas in the areas of responsibility, psychoanalysis, and understanding his own doubts and aesthetic conflicts. Walter thought that psychoanalysis was the art of memory; what struck him most was Freud's insistence that he forget about his arm. Walter thought Freud would see something infantile in his symptom and so relate it to sexuality, but Freud dismissed Walter's interpretation of psychoanalysis, just as he did with H.D. Most memorable was that Walter did not forget Freud's willingness to accept a responsibility that could never really be taken. That was how the analysis began and years later Walter (1966) wrote: "So by dint of much effort and confidence [in Freud], by learning and forgetting, I finally succeeded in finding my way back to my profession" (168).

NEGATIVE CAPABILITY

From these imaginative constructions made from the remnants of history, we glimpse the psychoanalytic problem of trying to understand the expressions and symbolization of internal plurality. What matters to living an artistic life is tolerating the unknown. The poet John Keats described such effort as "negative capability" (Forman 1960). He used that phrase in one of his letters written in 1817 as he tried to describe the artist's labor of imagination. In the language of his time he wrote: "I mean *Negative Capability*, that is when man is capable of being in uncertainties, Mysteries, doubts, without any irritable reaching after fact and reason" (71). I think all of the artists—H.D., Rilke, Walter, and Mahler—suffered a crisis of negative capability, one that threatened to destroy their creative work. There is a terrible confusion of doubts over the nature of beauty and goodness and anxious questions over the source of one's misery. There is a loss of hope that one's efforts can matter.

Earlier in this chapter, I raised the unanswerable question: where does creativity come from? The other side of the question concerns the origin of misery. If we consider only the world of others as the source of our misery and artistic failings, we are apt to fall into an impossible defense that Freud warned H.D. about, or else decide too soon what is important and unimportant. If we situate the external world as the only source of misery, as Jacqueline Rose (1993) has argued, the inner world becomes irrelevant, small, private, and either a privilege denied to others or simply a sign of narcissism. There is then no responsibility, for everything is ordained. Yet the external world is just as affected when the internal world is disavowed: it, too, becomes idealized, disparaged, and timeless. Paradoxically, the more we refuse our inner world in the name of rationality or politics, the more we feel its unimportance, the more rigid, timeless, and unforgiving reality becomes and the more lost, disparaged, or forgotten becomes our history. With the idea of negativity capability we are permitted the depth of emotional reality as capable of both registering the world that cannot be known and signifying how it is that we come to be affected. Keats's idea of negative capability holds open this empty space and leaves us our doubts and questions.

Meltzer and Williams (1988) expand Keats's negative capability with their idea of aesthetic conflict, an encounter with both beauty and violence: beauty of the object, violence in its capacity to be destroyed or to destroy. They asked about our agony: "How to live with a relatively harmonious inner world enriched by the bounty and beauty of one's good objects, in an outside world that mirrors its beauty but not its harmony, *about which one can no longer remain unconcerned?*" (ital. original, 221–222). Perhaps they are a bit too oblique although I felt this conflict as I walked through the Jewish Museum of Berlin. I think they are speaking both to an experience of responding to a work of art that is itself a representation of what the artist cares about *and* our ability to relate to that which is without art: difficult experiences of social despair, intolerance, and the breakdown of meaning. Negative capability would allow forming the terrifying question: how does the capacity to love beauty affect our encounters with intolerance?

By 1941, Bruno Walter was living in exile in the United States where he published an article titled, "About War and Music." In part he wrote:

> I wanted to make up my mind whether now, when the battle of humanity is being fought, music should be allowed to retain the same importance as before. I began to see that music does not mean escape from world affairs; it can, in fact, play an active role. . . . To cultivate those things which have given meaning to our lives. . . . The more decency and fair play are trampled underfoot by the enemy, the more faithfully should we observe them. The more tyrannically the other side perverts science and art, the more should we encourage a free art and a free science. (cited in Ryding and Pechefsky, 272–273)

There is no escape from world affairs and our emotional world registers this responsibility. And when the question of what is important and unimportant is raised, we can begin to see that what is most important is our capacity to respond to what is most difficult about freedom. With negative capability we may begin to understand that living in the world requires our response to the world and our responsibility in the world is affected by our having to symbolize the world.

MEMORY PROBLEMS AND THE CONSTRUCTION OF HISTORY

Testimony, we know, comes to us in so many forms: music, poetry, visual art, literature, memoirs, built things, and also historical records. And education, we know, receives its stammering. We are doubly affected: as we work with testimonies that affect us, the fault lines of our education are animated. How easily imagination and desire merge for the witness. And how difficult it becomes to extricate our drive to know from our desire to understand what has already happened to others but is inconceivable to us. What then is happening to what has already happened?

Ricoeur's (2004) lectures on history and forgetting raise the question of how we come to understand the truthful dimension of memory when memory and imagination are so difficult to separate. He asks, "Can the relation to the past be only a variety of *mimesis*?" (13). Yet a collapse of memory with imagination poses a paradox. Without imagination we cannot fantasize how others experienced events we could not have lived through. Nor could we place our own present in relation to the other's past. The work of imagination permits us this affected history. Still, imagination carries with it the distortions, repressions, and unconscious wishes that remix and confuse history with our own psychical life wishes and so render history timeless, like the unconscious. Here imagination fails through denial of painful events and a radical difficulty to believe the consequences of humanly created catastrophe as our inheritance. A failure of imagination is essentially a resistance to working through the past and thus a failure to mourn. Ricouer insists we have no other resource for knowing the past except someone's memory, which "signifies that something has taken place, has occurred, has happened *before* we remember it" (21). And he links this untimely time, an event before memory, to the question of the reception of testimony as our capacity to integrate loss with memory.

Reality, even if accepted, is not easily known. Elizabeth Rottenberg (2005) places the untimely time of the event before memory as a question of "inheriting the future" (xxi), a responsibility to respond. She believes that the giving and receiving of testimony is a psychological need: "human beings need to humanize impersonal forces and destinies that afflict them" (5). Yet this need to humanize begins with projections and negations, through disavowal of what is unpleasurable and indeed painful, what is inhuman. She makes the argument that the field of ethics turns to psychoanalysis not because the pleasure principle is so difficult to renounce but because of Freud's understanding of the reality principle: that the ego has the capacity to turn away from reality through its defenses. And she links this turning away from reality to the prohibition against thought and judgment, where just as the ego, in order to think, must take into itself that which is disagreeable but real, it can also take cover in its phantasies.

For Eric Santer (2001), the turn away from reality raises the problem of intolerance as both a defense against reality and memory. He, too, approaches memory as radically relational, rather than simply mimetic, and as untimely because memory, like imagination, is dependent on others and affected by the symbolic register, or the meanings that precede us. The tension is that memory is subject then to problems of authority and authorization and consequently, to education. This brings him to the problem of education's responsibility and to his critique of our pedagogical efforts to cure intolerance. We tend to historicize intolerance, situating it only in external conditions—differences between cultures, for example. What becomes unimaginable and intolerable is the idea that intolerance also has to do with a refusal to be affected by the other. This was Freud's point to H.D. when he reminded her never to defend psychoanalysis. Intolerance, Santer suggests, also constitutes identity itself since identity is subject to the drives, to excitability, perturbation, to phantasies, and to its own defensive structures. Drawing from Freud's view that humans are self-interpreting creatures, Santer proposes the problem we have with the symbolic. It is not just that our symbols are saturated with cultural meaning and that we merely take them in. The procedures of symbolization already carry a libidinal relationship. "In a certain sense," Santer writes, "psychoanalysis proper begins with the thought that human beings can suffer not only from this or that inhibition in one's behaviour but also the very way in which the world is disclosed to use from within, [what the poet Paul Celan calls]'our angle of inclination'" (39–40). That is, our inhibitions are a relation to what is intolerable in having to symbolize the ways the world is disclosed to us.

As I read these debates on testimony, memory, and responsibility, I was struck by the centrality of education as a public space for understanding and misunderstanding, by the collapse of so many pedagogic themes, and then by how I am affected in my own capacity to turn away from reality. Yet if pedagogy itself inherits this problem when, for example, students and teachers encounter testimonies of social discord, betrayal, and inhumanity, it may first need to pass through what is often inexpressible for us: our various phantasies that defend against reality. This may be what Ricoeur considered as an event before memory and what challenges our negative capabilities. In pondering these problems I encounter my own defenses as well; it has to do with my fascination with the year 1933, as if my own transference was unimportant.

Earlier I mentioned my encounter with the interview of Hannah Arendt that endlessly played on a television monitor in a corner of the Jewish Museum in Berlin. And just as Micha Ullman's monument "The Empty Library" was so easy for me to miss, so, too, was the little monitor in the museum. I had almost walked past it. That interview, I found out later, was published under the title "What Remains? The Language Remains."[6] I had in fact read this interview, but had forgotten it. Rereading the interview, what now struck me was how Arendt, only in retrospect, understood that the year 1933 was important *and* unimportant. It was important because that year she, too, with so many others, escaped Berlin to move to Paris where she worked for a Zionist agency sending Jewish youth to Palestine. That year was important both personally and politically in that Arendt said she became deeply disillusioned with the capitulation of some intellectuals, perhaps as the journalist Joseph Roth was. But the year was also unimportant when she said to the interviewer,

> You know, what was decisive was not the year 1933, at least not for me. What was decisive [in 1943] was the day we learned about Auschwitz. . . . And at first we didn't believe it . . . because militarily it was unnecessary and uncalled for. . . . It was really as if an abyss had opened. Because we had the idea that amends could somehow be made from everything else . . . but not for this. *This ought not to have happened.* . . . Something happened there to which we cannot reconcile ourselves. (Arendt, 2005, 13–14)

The year was unimportant because of what could not be known or believed and what still cannot be understood. I wonder if my own insistence on the importance of the year 1933 was a defense against what happened afterward, a foreclosure of memory's irreconcilable time, and thus an event before memory. I also wonder if my memory of the televised interview clip and my misquoting of it were affected, as I walked through the narrow, jagged, disorienting spaces of the Jewish Museum of Berlin, by my experience of feeling the losses of bodies each exhibit marked. Perhaps my misrecognition was a registration of an aesthetic conflict, that timeless moment when memory itself is caught within the need to keep the world as it was and the anxiety of its traumatic loss.

Education, too, is a place where the world is disclosed, not just when we meet our curriculum but in how this disclosure meets our own inclinations. Our proclivity for censorship and forgetting, our eschewal and even fear of affect, and our anxiety over the complicated, inchoate body, are, I think, symptoms of our failure of imagination. If as Ricoeur suggests, memory and imagination are so closely linked, and if, as Rottenberg reminds, testimony itself is a psychological need and so registers within identity a quality of the inhuman and its resistance to that quality, and if, as Santer insists, all these affects constitute and call forth defenses against what is intolerable, then the nature of our educational responsibility and its negative capability may be more difficult than we have ever imagined.

OUR PSYCHOANALYTIC CENTURY

Kristeva (2001) has audaciously named the twentieth century "Our Psycho-analytic Century" (5). We may see this century now as one preoccupied with affect, subjectivity, family, and narrative; a century of testimony and educa-tion, and a century of conflict, sublation, preservation, and of overcoming. But it is also the century of the return of the repressed, of archaic hatreds, of the repetition compulsion, of war, and of suffering, and the advent of the unconscious. Our psychoanalytic century returns what history has left us: the question of imagination and the difficulty of how education may disclose the world.

In the psychoanalytic clinic, learning and forgetting go hand in hand. Indeed, in one of his few papers on psychoanalytic technique, Freud (1914a) would describe the psychoanalytic process through its three modalities of communication: "repeating, remembering, and working through." His idea was that we repeat what is forgotten, yet the repetition, itself an attempt to master a traumatic perception, eludes our knowing it as such because the form it takes is resistance to remembering. In Freud's formulation: "we may say the patient does not remember anything of what he has forgotten and repressed, but acts it out. He reproduces it not as a memory but as an action; he *repeats* it, without, of course, knowing that he is repeating it" (150). Remembering is, for Freud, the work of the mind, an experimental means for placing an event into time that has already gone. More than historicization, remembering is also a libidinal tie, needed to symbolize absence. In a curious way, it gives us the freedom we bestow to the object. Working through memorializes these efforts, permitting imagination its capacity to symbolize the meaning of the past for today. What has already happened will not change, but we become transformed. Imagination is brought closer to the work of mourning, where we experience the relation between our history of resistance to self-under-standing and the loss of the other.

Loewald (2000b) has suggested that one of the greatest challenges each of us faces is to allow the past to be over in order for reality to be interpreted anew. His history also bore the shadow of World War II; he was once a student of Heidegger and was dismissed from the university because he was Jewish. Loewald left his philosophical studies in 1933 for exile, first going to Italy to study medicine and then to the United States where he practiced psychoanalysis. He, too, understood that what has passed cannot, after all, be changed. Rather, in psychoanalytic terms, the past leaves to us its excesses, what could not or would not be grasped at the time of the event but now must be symbolized. Loewald calls this work responsibility. And, with a change in grammar, he opens a psychological distinction between accepting responsibility for the past and taking responsibility for the past. Taking responsibility, Loewald implies, leads only to blame, guilt, and defenses against our inheritance. Accepting responsibility is to own, in the fullest sense, one's relation to the past, to accept responsibility for representing, indeed for symbolizing, a new approach to an old object. In his discussion on the repetition compulsion, Loewald (2000a) argues there is a mode of repeating that is moral and that gives birth to a self. And while Loewald may not have thought about Freud's analysis with Bruno Walter, I can see Freud's acceptance of a responsibility in Loewald's terms because Freud invited its symbolization. I think we can also see this acceptance of responsibility as an address to our first aesthetic conflict, where the mother's beauty and mystery call forth our minds and our worries over loss and where, as well, we have our first fair play.

One of the most provocative descriptions of psychoanalysis I have come across, one without defense, belongs to Jose Infante's (1995) view of psychoanalysis as "a therapy of fate" (61). Infante's formulation emerged as he considered Freud's short essay on creative writing and daydreaming, in which Freud could not really answer the question of where creativity comes from. Calling on the Oedipus myth, Infante suggests that a great deal of what goes on in the analytic sessions is an attempt to construct a new meaning from what could not be known at the time. Kristeva (1989) sees this as "the subject's battle with symbolic collapse" (24). Certainly this method of interpretation, this "therapy of fate," was one H.D. (2003) created in her haunting translation/ adaptation of Euripides' play, *Ion*. She completed this book around 1937, just a few years after her analysis with Freud but still in the time of war. I noted earlier that H.D. left her analysis in 1934 with her writing difficulties and her translation of Euripides' play can be considered as her working through of the analysis (Friedman 2002). In H.D.'s *Tribute to Freud*, we find his note of congratulation on the translation, thanking H.D. for introducing to him this Greek tragedy. *Ion*, in her hands, grapples with that tragic difference between the important and the unimportant, with what is forgotten but repeated, and then with working through the sorrow and loss made from remembering and so learning to speak freely.[7]

H.D.'s translation cannot be loyal to any originary moment, partly because the play poses a problem of origin, deception, and truth, partly because H.D. chose the genre of an adaptation, and partly because she desired Euripides' play, written around 418 B.C., to enliven our contemporary world by urging us to remember our unconscious. So many ideas are noteworthy here, including how this ancient play becomes, in her hands, "ultra modern" (172), and a means for testimony to take residence in what is enigmatic for inner and external worlds. Through her transference, time is confused, events come before memory. Words are the transfer points for readers to move between antiquity and modernity: we see the tension made when the wish for rhapsodic peace meets the terror of contemporary war. Ever the analyst, H.D. gives us some instructions as to how to read the play, which she has arranged in eighteen sections separated by her commentary. She advises readers, before considering her words, to read the play through to its ending. But we cannot follow her advice since her commentary is also the play. Here again one can find her interest with the analysis of unconscious worlds, with what occurs beneath speech, with what cannot be put into speech and is acted out before it can be remembered. Here, too, we may find H.D.'s transference people: the boy, the woman, the poet, the Greek chorus, and then something lovingly abstract: the affected semiotics and the affected poet. And in her coda, written almost twenty years after the translation, she insists that readers be affected by the untimely time of imagination: "*Today, again at a turning-point in the history of the world, the mind stands, to plead, to condone, to explain, to clarify, to illuminate . . . each one of us is responsible to that abstract reality. . . . What now will we make of it?*"(255, ital. original).

What now will we make? Education is where the world is disclosed and where minds must plead, argue, and exchange aesthetic conflicts. This urges education into something unknown even as it must accept responsibility for responding to events before memory. But this means education, too, occupies the space of a therapy of fate. To accept this imagination, education will have to suspend its defensive insistence on what is important and unimportant; it will have to accept responsibility for its disclosure of words and things and for symbolizing our negative capabilities. Indeed, our education will have to learn to respond to its own unknown as it also destroys the defenses made from what we know too well.

CHAPTER SEVEN

THE IMPOSSIBLE PROFESSIONS

School life also gives opportunity for a greater separation of hate
from love than was possible in the small family circle. At school,
some children can be hated, or merely disliked, while others can
be loved. In this way, both repressed emotions of love and hate—
repressed because of the conflict about hating a loved person—can
find fuller expression in a more or less socially accepted direction.

—Melanie Klein, "Love, Guilt and Reparation"

While not explicitly addressing the impossible professions, Klein proposes that
our emotional ties expand when we add to the fray the additional factor of
education. Look and see what else happens when we go to school. Life in
school is a veritable carnival of projective identifications and there are ample
opportunities for love and hate to grow into ideas and new projects. While
Klein imagined this education as providing a new emotional playground for
children, we don't often understand the adult's education as also providing an
occasion for diffusing love and hate. What may be forgotten in this transference neurosis—education's own artificial illness—is the way love and hate
animate the adult's phantasies of the educational frame. This corner of the
impossible professions is deeply defended since it reaches into the internal
conflicts the professions would rather disclaim. Can the impossible professions learn to tolerate their own internal conflicts—their love and hate—and
analyze their education? Freud gives us a glimpse of what one is up against

when he suggested education as one of the impossible professions. The term "impossible" has emotional impact and it turns out that the very thought of the impossible professions takes us into the heart of our educational neuroses.

Freud's (1925c) first mention of "the impossible professions" found in his preface to August Aichhorn's educational text *Wayward Youth* addresses the field of education. He may have worried what educators would make of this association, whether our feelings might be hurt. So he concludes with an assurance: "At an early stage I had accepted the *bon mot* which lays it down that there are three impossible professions—educating, healing and governing—and I was already fully occupied with the second of them. But this does not mean that I overlook the high social value of the work done by those of my friends who are engaged in education" (273). Let us note that Freud's assurance to educators comes wrapped in a negation, a statement that says, "but this does not mean that . . ." or "It's not what I think." Should we then suppose that the very thought of education causes disturbance?

That same year, Freud (1925b) published an article on negation describing its work as "a way of taking cognizance of what is repressed; indeed, it is already a lifting of the repression, although not, of course, an acceptance of what is repressed" (235–236). Repression is one of the many defenses of the ego that services the gap between the unconscious and the conscious. With it, the ego tries to solve a conflict between an unacceptable idea and its affective force by doing away with the idea. To read these two articles together, one can ask: If it is so well known that education is an impossible profession, then why is it so emotionally difficult to accept? Freud's negation—"but this does not mean that"—in his preface to Aichhorn's book may give us a clue. In listening to this affected speech, one takes away "the no" to learn something more about the nature of the objection. What might be revealed in looking over our high social value? And, if negation signals "a lifting of repression," can returning the emotional force to the original idea of the impossible professions herald education's therapeutic action?

Freud (1925a) also published what we may think of today as a short companion piece to both essays, carrying the title "Resistances to Psychoanalysis." It gives us another clue as to how we are affected by what the impossible professions demand of us. There, he points out that the strongest resistance to this second impossible profession, often cloaked in an intellectual objection, is really an emotional reaction against psychoanalysis: "The majority of [resistances to psychoanalysis] are due to the fact that powerful human feelings are hurt by the subject matter of theory" (221). Theory itself hurts our feelings and also may carry a defense against having our feelings hurt. This leads Freud to the question of philosophy, which also burdens itself with this dual function. Its feelings will also be hurt by psychoanalysis because philosophy invests in the idea of the observing ego as the sum total of mental life and so it, too, runs into the problem of narcissism. To begin elsewhere is to point out that the ego's perceptions are already influenced by what it does not want to know, including its mechanisms of defense against anxiety such as intellectualization, repression, negation, and resistance. Again, the powerful feelings both hurt and protected belong to the ego's narcissism.

Throughout this essay on resistance, Freud (1925a) persists in hurting feelings, listing three theories that incur a narcissistic blow: psychoanalysis provides a psychological blow to human narcissism, prior to that was Darwin's theory, which constitutes a biological blow, and earlier than that, a cosmological blow occurs with Copernicus's theory (221). These theories challenge feelings that sustain and idealize self-regard, agency, and omnipotence. Each theory supposes that everything once felt as true and intuitive must be questioned and exchanged for something far more disturbing and uncertain. Yet giving up the pleasures of certainty create particular problems for conceptualizing education in the impossible professions since certainty, or the doing away of difference, is one of the hallmarks of narcissism. What can the impossible professions make of these terrible blows since each theory asserts human meaning as in conflict with its need for certainty, that ideas will attempt to ward off the chaos of life and death, and that our theories originate from, repeat, and defend against the trauma of human existence? What are we to make of the problem that, when we try to approach our narcissistic inventions, which also seem like a good idea, narcissism is hurt?

Freud's formulation of the impossible professions may still feel like a blow to our professional narcissism. Surely the charge of narcissism is affecting since the impossible professions take pride in their altruism, or their neutrality, or their objectivity. In pointing out the problem of narcissism, we are on the verge of exposing what is most subjective, protected, and fragile about ourselves as we work. Analysis excites doubt over our ideals and may challenge our libidinal investment in such things as status, certitude, the legitimization of measures, and may even crush our ambitions for science. The charge returns us to our own unwelcome excess, the ways in which we do not give up our libidinal pleasures easily, but also how love turns into hate, or suffers in its loss, and the onslaught of deceptions made when we fixate on our conscious intentions. The idea of an impossible profession affects us because it proposes a constitutive discontinuity, a lack the profession represses, negates, and projects into others. The impossible professions are a terrible remainder of what is most incomplete, arbitrary, and archaic in us and in the events of working with others. We may be returned to the chaos of experience, our first impossibility, what Agamben (2007) in his investigation of the nonrelation between knowledge and experience provocatively calls "infancy." We may be subject to our own revolting questions, themselves a precursor to therapeutic action.

There is something ironic about narcissism, to say nothing about its own particular impossibility. The impossible professions have their own gigantic share, yet, without self-regard, the subject would be nothing. Narcissism, however, is not without ambivalence since perfection is impossible and since it is so easily crushed and susceptible to depressive illness where nothing seems to matter at all. Can the impossible professions give a good account of their depressive qualities? How might we think our quest for love and our desire for knowledge as affecting our own educational imaginary?

The subjective, affected world of education involves the impossible professions with what love and knowledge signify there. The paradox is that while love and knowledge may well be our cause, together they create the links of the social bond and the agony made when bonds are broken. Our relations with love and knowledge are also where we feel most incomplete, lonely, and alienated. And they electrify what is most private yet nonetheless expressed, namely, our emotional situation conveyed by our passion, phantasy, projective identification, resistance, transference, and even empathy. These primary experiences are the means for introjecting and projecting affectivity: opening life to modes for caring for the self, and expelling what is hated in the self into the world and therefore communicating distress by evading anxiety. Through these procedures, we witness and negate enigmatic subjectivity. They are also the emotional means for understanding, misunderstanding, and for tolerating not understanding, subtle events that compose our moment-to-moment education (Joseph 1997).

Readers are asked to keep in mind this affected world of subjectivity as our first impossibility so that we can explore with psychoanalytic interest the impossible professions' affective logic, beginning with phantasies of education. This direction will advance a general commentary on learning difficulties within the impossible professions. My speculation is that learning in the impossible professions is the Achilles' heel of our education, by which I mean the culmination of an area of vulnerability and uncertainty that we defend against in the name of qualifications and high social value. The chapter blends clinical, philosophical, and literary discussion to suggest that a large impossibility we all share is the problem of symbolizing experience in education. Bion (2000) called this subjective play—the inevitable drama when people meet—"emotional storms" (321). Why the impossible professions have such difficulty claiming their affected experience in education is one part of the story. The other part has to do with instituting education itself and whether we might imagine the experience of learning within the impossible professions as an encounter with what is most subjective and intimate about finding our selves with others. Indeed, if education is our transference playground of love and hate, learning one's emotional situation provides the means for tolerating the very thought of this education. With the idea of the impossible professions, the heart of this chapter explores the problem of how education, as the transference of desire for knowledge and love, may be transformed into a capacity to tolerate uncertainty. While subjectivity is there without the impossible professions, the impossible professions cannot do without their subjectivity.

RESISTANCE

We should admit from the onset that representing the force of our subjectivity is no easy matter and theory itself gives us this clue. In his "Resistances to Psychoanalysis," Freud (1925a) picks on what a philosophy forgets. Critical theory, too, has its points of forgetting even as it teaches us how historically saturated any representation of subjectivity must be. Its index is dazzling. What is missing, however, is how critical theory understands learning—why the subject learns at all, how it is so susceptible to aggression, violence, language, and to its own inhibitions, for instance, and what it does with itself because of what others do to it. Typically, subjectivity is approached as the container of external events, themselves formed by social procedures such as ideology, consumerism, information, and prejudice. Yet this does not solve the old question Ruti (2006) brings to the fore: "How shall I live?" (1). While learning critical theory is an entirely different matter and commentaries on learning this theory are found in the published lectures of Foucault (2005) and Adorno (2001), for example, the desire for love and the quest for knowledge as the revelatory learning, are overlooked. And we hardly ask that other question: "How shall I learn?" These are the absences that impoverish our capacity to consider the creative source of subjectivity or ponder its impressive nature. To acknowledge our capacity for depth and phantasy as an outcome of love and knowledge would mean that something about us couldn't be predicted, controlled, or prevented. And this depth psychology challenges the narcissistic foundations of the impossible professions.

In the archive of critical theory, one finds subjectivity cataloged as structure, as subjection, as an effect of discourse, as constructed, as suggestible, and as supposition (Copjec 1994). There are claims of history without origin: that subjectivity is a modern invention or is always essentially there (Foucault 2005). There are arguments in favor of its unaccountability (Butler 2005). Subjectivity is subject to its own multiplicity and divisions, to conditions of culture and language, to power and knowledge, and to what is illogical about the hermeneutic circle (Butler 1997). Agency, too, will find its cul de sac in its myths of grandiosity, in solipsism, in the monad, and in abjection or perversion (Kristeva 1982). We meet fallibility through the Cartesian subject who turns doubts into certainty, in the postmodern subject who performs again and again, and in the potential space of *Da-Sein,* who somehow throws itself into being there (Frie 2003). There, too, lurks the tragic Kantian figure, the "I think that accompanies all of my representations" who bumps up against its aporia, the Kantian block that Adorno (2001) eulogies as "a kind of metaphysical mourning, a kind of memory of what is best, of something we must not forget, but that we are nevertheless compelled to forget" (176). It will be left to psychoanalysis to explore our historicity as an echo of our neotenic condition: that we are born immature, that the need we have for the other fuses with the demand for love and the other's knowledge, that sexuality inaugurates the beginning of sensate life, and that the human, the slowest creature to mature, is subject to regression to an earlier state and so to mental breakdown, to the ecstasy of creativity, and to the enigmatic message of others. We are compelled to forget these experiences, our own Freudian block, so to speak.

These theoretical subjects, however, can only begin in their own education. Our subjectivity, after all, is parented and education itself is its own Oedipal complex. The child is always with adults who seem to know and every adult was once a child who needed this mysterious knowledge. From the beginning of life there is the breast that links what is enigmatic in objects to the advent of Eros, phantasy, infantile sexual theory, and symbolization (Klein 1930). This dreamy progression of love and knowledge may give us clues as to why, when subjectivity staggers, there is loss, melancholia, narcissistic injury, anxiety, and a lowering of self-regard, or why, in its expansiveness, there is overvaluation, narcissistic completion, omnipotence, manic triumphalism, and bliss. And perhaps these human extremes cannot be otherwise since subjectivity is always subject to both its drives and to what is uncanny in their worldly representation. Subjectivity's own condition, having to interpret unknown reality and the other's unconscious, is always at stake. And learning itself suffers from this radical indeterminacy.

Our theories, too, repeat this strange malaise in that theory itself can never quite say why we have theory at all. This aporia follows from Laplanche's (1999) critique of what he sees as missing from psychoanalysis: "analytic theory ought to help us understand the status of theory itself" (118). For Laplanche, the exemplary theory that neither knows its own reason nor its duration is infantile sexual theory made from the desire to know one's origin. What follows is that any theory will be an attempt to bind the enigmatic message of the other. But this then means that our attempts to make, learn, or apply theory carries out an erotic quality, what Lacan (1998a), bringing us back to the question of education, describes as "a passion for ignorance" (121). It can seem as if we do not want to know why we have theory.

These subjective events pose profound difficulties for education and education has always posed problems for psychoanalysis. Can there be an education for analysts that can exceed education's neurotic, psychotic, and perverse trends? Can there really be a psychoanalytic education, an education that can analyze its own unfolding? Freud needed education to introduce the impossible professions, yet in admitting education's strange admixture of influencing and being influenced, psychoanalysis would need to distinguish itself from it, but not be so far away that its own educational limits would be ignored through acting out (Britzman 2003a). If the key concepts of psychoanalysis challenge the empirical world and the thinker's motivations in understanding and not understanding, what would be the ground of the psychoanalyst's learning? The gigantic problem is whether the very thought of this education can be put in the service of therapeutic action.

THIS IS NOT A THEORY

We can glimpse the magnitude of this educational dilemma—that is, the problem of what specifically is therapeutic or pedagogical about our actions—through controversies over the status of psychoanalytic theory and its clinical practice. Can one event really lead into another? Where would one locate transformation or meaningful change? Can measures of experience stabilize the radical unknown of the unconscious? This conflict may well be a consequence of the psychoanalytic field since psychoanalysis may be the only theoretical and practical intervention that turns its inceptions—the primary one being the unconscious and its resistance to being known—back upon itself. But this means that both theory and practice begin with the analyst's latency or ignorance and learning one's own latency as one is in the midst of it requires not only techniques that can tolerate not understanding but an interest in questioning how and why experience and reality come to matter. "Analysis," writes the philosopher Sarah Kofman (2007a) in her essay on this impossible profession, "does not fit into any preexisting techne, even if most of the arts can serve as its metaphoric models" (61). When thinking through Freud's advice on learning the profession of psychoanalysis, she wonders whether in fact psychoanalysis is a profession at all, or whether it can only be expressed with the irony of Magritte's painting of a pipe whose words negates the image of a pipe. Kofman then comments: "This is Not a Profession" (56). The techniques of psychoanalysis are not instructions, cannot really be taught, but are themselves instructive. Psychoanalytic technique is an event before memory, affecting both the meanings of learning and the subject who learns. All of this transference alters the analyst's sense of becoming. In Kofman's view, what is impossible about this profession is also its best irony: analysis attempts to handle the uncontrollable through play.

The analyst can only approach the circulation of knowledge and love through phantasy and the detours of free association. The term used to contain what is inexpressible and insistent about this exchange of love and knowledge—what is most influential and combustible for the analytic couple—is the impressive transference. Indeed, the history of psychoanalysis as deferred action is always affected by psychoanalytic process. History as well is latency and so is no longer something to be uncovered since it carries, as Copjec (1994) argues, "a simple impossibility: *no historical moment can be comprehended in its own terms.* . . . This impossibility causes each historical moment to flood with alien, anachronistic figures, spectres from the past and harbingers of the future" (ix). The impossibility is uncanny and these archaic figures confused in time and propelled by anxiety present what is inexpressible in the anticipation of the historical moment. The impossibility is that the transference, too, is both resistance to history and means for history to be retroactively constructed, questioned, and symbolized.

Now wait just a minute, readers may be thinking. How can the transference be both resistance and the means to its overcoming? So, here, let us pause for an intellectual objection. Many critics consider psychoanalysis as caught in its own miserable teleology. They argue that if resistance to psychoanalysis is located in the unknowing ego, where the ego cannot know its own mechanisms of defense, does not this view of the subject, which only psychoanalysis proposes, create the resistance that is then confirmed by its order of psychoanalytic knowledge? The objections are that psychoanalysis is deterministic as opposed to existential, that it causes the transference that it then interprets, and that psychoanalysis invents identification with the psychoanalytic object. These objections collapse with the psychoanalytic view of temporality, psychical working over, and deferred action. Psychoanalytic temporality is recursive, overdetermined by our capacity for revision and what undergoes translation is not the experience but what experience could not mean at the time of its impact. Apprehension of the meanings of life's events can only be made retroactively: narratives from present knowledge animated by a memory fold back into itself and therefore affect the current significance of past events. The story childhood tells of itself are those of an adult looking back at what could not be understood at the time and this temporality means, among other things, that we are at our most impressive when we do not know.

Yet the more one argues with psychoanalysis, the more emotionally entangled one becomes and the more psychoanalysis seems to enjoy the objection. Indeed, psychoanalysis depends upon enlivening emotional life, our susceptibility to the other, and our capacity to passionately attach our love to anything or anyone for no reason at all. However, these objections take us to one of the conflicts the techne effectuates, noticed by Kofman (2007a) when she turned psychoanalysis around to act on itself. If psychoanalysis, too, is subject to the transference, how can the field interpret its own transference? What would be the future of its own critique?

Near the end of his career, Freud (1937) attempted to analyze the psychoanalytic field with a concept he called "resistance to resistance" (239). He also returned to the idea of psychoanalysis as the second impossible profession where, given its constitution, he concludes "one can be sure beforehand of achieving unsatisfying results" (248). This essay tries to specify when analysis is over. But the problem of cure leads Freud back to the analyst who will fail, particularly if the analyst has expectations and a plan to impose. Freud's admission leads to two significant tensions, one having to do with the analyst's qualifications and the other with the limits of psychoanalysis. Notably, the problem of endings and qualifications brings Freud back to education: he questions the analyst's translation of psychoanalytic education and even the nature of education as such. Essentially, the impossibility of the professions leads Freud to the impossibility of their education.

As for the analyst's qualifications, Freud understands this education as interminable: "But where and how is the poor wretch to acquire the ideal qualifications which he will need in his profession? . . . in an analysis of himself" (248). Even this affected education cannot escape the impossible professions since education itself may deceive and its powers misused. What can it mean, after all, for one impossible profession to anchor itself in another impossible profession? Freud was pessimistic whether psychoanalysis could overcome its own education and learning psychoanalysis would be the Achilles' heel of psychoanalysis, just as learning to be an educator would be for education. Can any of the impossible professions escape the compliance, paranoia, and destruction of questions, which also occur under the name of education? The second tension is related to the limits of analysis, another aspect of education. How can one conceptualize the force of resistance to resistance without claiming a transcendental ego and thereby reinstituting a centered and unified subject? What could be the other side of resistance? More resistance, it turns out, but, this time, from the analyst's side.

The analyst's resistance to resistance, what Derrida (1998) justly called "resistances of psychoanalysis," is a remarkable, irreducible dimension of subjectivity. There is no chance of unifying resistance through the ideas of ego, defense, repetition compulsion, the drives, or the transference, since psychical reality is discordance and since no one escapes the force of the dynamic unconscious, itself defined by what resists or what is not known. Indeed, the other side of this impossibility goes under the name of therapeutic action, also accompanying resistance but now as a form of working through. This resistance, as Derrida argues, brings psychoanalysis to its own Kantian block: "when one seeks to determine the unity of this concept . . . one encounters a "resistance to analysis" that figures *both* the most resistant resistance, resistance par excellence, hyperbolic resistance, *and* the one that disorganizes the very principle, the constitutive idea of psychoanalysis as analysis of resistances" (22). The curious and difficult qualities of psychoanalytic practice concern the fact that the analyst, too, is affected by her or his transference and the form it will take is the transference, an unconscious exchange of knowledge and love but also hatred and aggression. The analyst is affected by her or his resistance that must place self-knowledge into doubt. This disorganization may lead to the analyst's question of whose resistance is at stake in the psychoanalytic field. It may also lend new meaning to the impossible profession, but now from the vantage of what is impossible about self-analysis.

Like education, psychoanalysis is an affected science, if we mean by science a capacity to present new conceptualizations that can revitalize how we approach old dilemmas and impasses in thought and if we mean by affect, a capacity to be impressed with such feelings as pleasure, anxiety, and displeasure as we go about our work. André Green (1999) proposes the work of affect as "an encounter between the effects of the tensions aroused by the object and the event . . . not only the limit of their effects, but at one and the same time, a zone of interpenetration and a point of turning back. . . . affect is a time of revelation" (226). In its potential to register and repudiate differentiation, the affect's oscillations are revealed. Alan Bass (2000), in his inquiry into resistance to interpretation, posits this event as "the trauma of Eros": while love animates the individual, it is also where loss of love is simultaneously effectuated. Contact itself is feared. Interpretation services this difficult function, introducing or loosening the opposition affect contains but also incurring an excess of meaning. What the interpretation proposes is not the meaning of the affect, but an invitation to association and then to analyze its processive function as it plays out in the analytic relation (151). Here is where science is most affected because the problem becomes not so much what belongs to affect, for affect itself is belonging, but rather the wager is with affect as revelatory potential. Here is where affected science may internalize its own subjectivity.

Affected science is also a creature of culture. Both education and psychoanalysis signify their procedures: the work is conducted in language and silence, both are intersubjective endeavors, and again and again both posit their own dilemmas for understanding, misunderstanding, and not understanding. As in culture, both professions repeat a constitutive asymmetry made through the play of registration, difference, repudiation, and perhaps significance. What separates the function of education and psychoanalysis, however, is that even as psychoanalysis bears procedures of culture, it may aspire to create experiences beyond culture's dictate of adaptation. In its most radical potential psychoanalysis is against adaptation. Christopher Bollas (cited in Molino 1997) pointed to our significant problem with reality: we cannot adapt to it since reality is always complex reality and is therefore "unavailable for adaptation" (49). The tension is that reality is always interpreted reality and so will contain its own unknown and our resistance to that.

This unknown reality is deepened by the event of our singularity that structures and is structured by the movements of love, knowledge, and our questions. Joyce McDougall (1995) celebrates this diversity: "The remarkable aspect of human beings in their psychic structure—as in their genetic structure—is their singularity" (172). Singularity, itself without qualification, will pressure what we come to imagine as cure. McDougall advocates for an "open ethic of psychic survival" (224), which lends to resistance a new meaning. She proposes that if psychoanalysis is to affect its own ethics, if the analyst is to resist imposing her or his values onto the scene of shared phantasy and work against normalization and objectification, then therapeutic action should be thought of as that which sustains and expresses the creativity of psychic survival and include in this work the analysis of how it may be destroyed. This second movement is where education may be questioned: how does education destroy its potential? An open ethic of education involves a push toward creativity and a critique of what in this push may stop it short.

THE TRANSFERENCE

Was it really a coincidence that Freud first mentions the impossible professions in Aichhorn's (1983) *Wayward Youth*? Or was he trying to say something emotionally difficult about our education? Wayward youth are those who rebel, lose their way, or become so overwhelmed by what the society demands of them that they return these demands as the tantrums they feel them to be. These wayward youth are subjected to all three impossible professions. They run away, break the law, steal and lie, refuse to go to school, and destroy relationships. They are hard to pin down. They are impossible youth whose solution to distress is to cause more of it. They possess the uncanny capacity to induce adult rigidity and its perverse reply of needing to teach a lesson. Aichhorn presents this education as an Oedipal conflict. It is a situation not so different from the state of the impossible professions. All have their wayward tendencies: of repeating the internal conflict they attempt to address, of eschewing critique, and of displacing doubt into others. This is the other impossibility that the professions disclaim, which may be why Freud's approach was to return the negated critique back to us, as if to say that there can be no psychoanalysis without a critique of psychoanalysis, no education without a critique of education, and no government without a critique of government.

In bringing the impossible professions to their radical indeterminacy, Freud would confront a necessary failure of love and knowledge, something tragic in the human condition. But he also supposed that the professional's learning would always be out of joint. Defenses against not knowing would be a feature of these professions since they too belong to both historical reality and psychical reality. Such agony plays within the impossible profession even as the professions have a tendency to destroy identification with this anguish by objectifying its subjects without really knowing why. Lacan (1998a), we have seen, named this mystification "the passion for ignorance" (121). Even if we admit this otherness in our ongoing education—that it is difficult for the human to think otherwise than what it wants to know, or consider what else occurs when something occurs in the mind—even if we admit arbitrariness and accidents as setting the time of our work, our admission will not settle an understanding of what resists and invokes claiming the unknown as the central feature of subjectivity. Our subjectivity lends to this transference its poignancy and urgency, our means of both needing and not wanting to know.

Surely here we can feel a sigh of ambivalence, for we need to communicate not only a lost history of missed encounters and our dreams for them, but also our present currents of loving and hating. In this view, every affect is transference, a commentary of our bodies and our relations to others (Bird 1990). In this view, too, there can be no life, no love, no thinking, without the transference (Loewald 2000b).

The transference raises a particular dilemma for the impossible professions since learning itself is tied to the revelation of affect. The clinic of psychoanalysis, after all, reminds us that when push comes to shove, so to speak, the analyst's appeals to reality or to explanations of symptoms cannot, in and of themselves, become the basis of cure. Information, while interesting, may only invoke compliance or disbelief. For Lacan (1998b), the transference indicates the split subject. He considers the transference as signifying an "area of loss . . . a certain deepening of obscurantism, very characteristic of the condition of man in our times of supposed information—obscurantism which, without really knowing why"(127). It is both a loss and a defense against it, so, in Lacan's view, transference is where "doubt is recognized as certainty" (126) and where a closing up occurs. To open again, the subject must be touched, affected by the differentiating qualities of words (Fink 2002). The tension, however, is that language, too, indicates an absence and falls short in what it can say. There may be too many words or not enough, we don't want to listen, we already know that, or, through the protection of negation, we may deny being affected by the other. And resistance to interpretation plays both ways since the force of the affect is resisted by the idea of affect's meanings. The analyst's contribution can feel to the patient as interference that the analyst may then experience as a narcissistic blow. Just when something seems so theoretically right and here, too, is the transference, our ideas alone, even the most practical ones, cannot be the sine quo non of communication.

The analyst's urge to interpret, then, is subject to psychoanalysis. Winnicott's (1986b) understanding of his need to interpret brings in the other side of the resistance, whether it is situated in a need for disillusionment or in hatred in the countertransference. Winnicott certainly lends a different flavor to Freud's worry that the analyst's efforts will lead to unsatisfactory results, for Winnicott considers mistakes in the form of the analyst's fallibility as a sign of hope. His solution is to analyze his own efforts and he tells us he gives interpretations for two reasons:

(1) If I make none the patient gets the impression that I understand everything. In other words, I retain some outside quality by not being quite on the mark—or even by being wrong.

(2) Verbalization at exactly the right moment mobilizes intellectual forces . . .
    I never use long sentences unless I am very tired. If I am near exhaustion
    point I begin teaching. Moreover, in my view an interpretation containing
    the word "moreover" is a teaching session. (167)

Winnicott feels his mistakes as needed proof of the failure of the analyst's
omnipotence and as evidence of his difference from the analysand. But there
is also the analyst's hate and fear. The idea of hate in the countertransference, or the emotional response to the burden of practicing in an impossible
profession, is Winnicott's (1992) great contribution for the analyst's education. It can be linked as well to the problem of teaching: whenever I hate
my students, I teach without them. As for analysis, teaching sessions may
indicate the analyst's loss of hope and patience needed to maintain "some
outside quality."

   We can begin to see how education comes to be understood as the working through of the procedures of knowledge, whether these refer to techne
or psychical affectivity. Its impossibility does not so much reside in the sense
of its events but rather in what eludes the experience of education. When
Freud warned that psychoanalysis couldn't realize itself and that its techne
would repeat the problem it attempted to grasp, he introduced difference—
a lack—into its own identity. As for education, it, too, would be subject to
the transference and to repeating the learning problems it attempts to solve.
While normative views of education promise a progression of knowledge and
an accumulation of best practice, seen from the idea of resistance to education
or what education resists, the promise of education begins with the transference and its difference.

   The impossible professions ask a great deal of us, which may be one reason why we must first say yes and no to them. The invitation, too, is difficult:
to think without the Hegelian absolute and its illusion that knowledge can
dialectically resolve its constitutive vulnerability and so become unified and
whole. We are asked to question the romance of our measures and ponder
what escapes meaning. We are urged to consider what else occurs when we
feel certain and without our questions, or, as Lacan (1998a) put it, try to notice
the "equation of thought and that which is thought of" (105) as a symptom
of inhibition or closure. We are asked to consider the fundamental fantasy of
development without mistaking this wish for progress with the thing itself.
We are asked to ponder our narcissistic defenses. We are invited to wonder
why we have theory at all and we are urged to work from our ignorance.

   What is left to think is the impossibility of our work, not so much from
the place of its failure or the adequacy of technique but rather from within

the areas of conflict, where our work is most incomplete, and where we are surprised by what we do not really know. I take heart from how Richard Polk (2006), in his description of Heidegger's idea of inceptive thinking, described this work as "tentative and incomplete—a way for perpetual beginners" (125). Yet I also believe that we need to understand much better how difficult it is to think of oneself as always beginning, specifically in the contexts of learning the impossible professions where we feel placed or may feel we need to place ourselves in the opposite position of "the subject supposed to know." This impressive, narcissistic phantasy originates in the child's relation to the parent and persists in the transference to knowledge, authority, and love. It is also that which instituted education itself sustains at great cost to its creative potential.

A CLINICAL FRAGMENT

While Freud brought the idea of the impossible professions to their radical indeterminacy, the structural and emotional force of learning from this uncertainty is daunting. This kind of learning welcomes and relies on our personal conflict, what is most unresolved about having to learn. The new problem is to imagine one's psychic survival as desire. Recall that McDougall's (1995) open ethic of psychic survival linked creativity to the critique of that which destroys it. We can elaborate this open ethic, where the content is under construction, by way of a clinical fragment. I draw on a few sessions in my psychotherapeutic practice where I found myself and my patient surprised by something we knew nothing about, namely, what it feels like to symbolize the uncertainties of impossible professions. "Mr. B" was a graduate student working toward his doctoral degree. We met weekly in psychotherapy over three years. He sought psychoanalytic psychotherapy after becoming disillusioned with the rituals and routines of cognitive behavioral therapy. Mr. B explained that he suffered from panic attacks while trying to teach his students and now wanted to understand them.

Mr. B is learning to become a university professor. It is something, he says, that he always wanted to become, but worries whether he can teach in front of students since it is in the classroom where he experiences his panic attacks. In the beginning of our therapeutic work, he would report each week on the panic's arrival or delay: initially it came regularly, took his breath away, stopped all sense of time, and cut off his thoughts. He had a number of rituals to prevent these attacks, but the rituals themselves reminded him of the panic and its dangers. When Mr. B described what he worried would happen while teaching his students, he could only imagine running out of the classroom, or, even worse, crumbling to the floor as his students watch him lose his mind, the enigmatic resource needed to become a university professor. Sometimes his anxiety would erupt when the question he asked his students was met by their silence; when things went well, his thoughts might wander into this dangerous territory, as if daring an enemy to strike. In more than a few of our sessions we both speculated whether the class might invite his panic so that he will dismiss them a few minutes early. But when, on good days, the panic refused to show up, he worried that letting down his guard and thinking that all could be well would be the condition of the panic's return. So, for much of the time, Mr. B stands guard against himself, but, in doing so, finds it difficult to become the teacher he desires to be. And he worried that he cannot be a university professor if he cannot even stand in front of a class, if he can't stand teaching.

After months of exploring the microscopic movements of the panic's procedures, bodily disruptions, and affective geography, we both felt the futility of our efforts in situating a precipitating factor. Stories of origin will not be useful; the panic seems to come from nowhere. I began to wonder if the topic itself—our relentless tracking of the elusive panic—was making us nervous and that somehow, with our incessant examination, we were following along the symptom's footsteps, almost as if the therapy itself had become the bad classroom. Yet unable to leave this class, in one session it occurred to me to invite his thoughts on teaching and what he imagined the teacher's work entailed.

I learn that the teacher is an authoritative figure who always knows what to do, what to say, and so never experiences conflict, headaches, nausea, or anxiety. Oddly, the teacher is the perfect narcissist. This phantom figure never experiences awkward moments because the teacher knows all that there is to know about teaching before stepping into the class. The teacher is so perfect that he doesn't need to use any teaching techniques and in this phantasy the students soak up the teacher's superb knowledge as well as admire his absolute command. I know this teacher well. Its image has taunted me for years. Mr. B, too, understands this phantasy as one that agonizes and excites him. It functions to chastise him for the uncertainty he feels while teaching and promises a teaching without conflicts. I feel I am about to step onto my own thin ice, for if I offer any advice on what a teacher is or does or idealize my experience as a model to emulate, I, too, engage my own narcissistic phantasies and be caught in the tidal wave of the transference. I would also assume the position of the authority that torments him, my identification with the aggressor. In these helpless feelings and my defenses against them, in the transference/countertransference nexus, I begin to notice my need to have a teaching session and say, "moreover." I find myself wanting to help Mr. B out of the phantasy but then wonder if this desire is a part of the phantasy. So, I, too, am uncertain and I stay with what is slippery in our relationship, with what I do not know. I wonder aloud about psycho-analysis, sometimes known for wrecking authority by questioning the veracity of certainty. I say: "Isn't it funny that Freud called teaching one of the impossible professions? It really is impossible." We both felt relief that our respective impossibilities were not a private sentence but a feature of our relationship. And whereas the idea of the impossible professions may to lead us into critique, in this instance, it opened emotional contact needed for symbolization and creativity in the therapy. We could leave the classroom together.

That teaching and learning incur emotional upset, that we teach when we don't want contact, or that we worry the contact will crush is neither news to anyone learning to teach nor original for those who live its travails. That we are affected by the act of learning itself, however, is a condition that meets education's passion for ignorance. Learning animates projections of our internal world of object relations and defenses against them through bodily communication: panic attacks, lack of nerve, loss of words, or what is more commonly thought of as stage fright. Who wouldn't be scared by the subject presumed to know that, more often than not, takes the form of education itself? Symbolizing bodily affects are rarely considered as relevant to learning or to teaching. It may be because both knowledge and the teacher's body are depersonalized or because there is something about learning and teaching, something about being educated that is hard to stand or even admit. There is something abject about our work that feels like a personal defeat (Britzman 2006). Indeed, Kristeva (1982) suggests that feelings of abjection are "a kind of narcissistic crisis: it is witness to the ephemeral aspect of the state called narcissism" (14) that implies not just fragility but loss itself, an absence that may inaugurate and destroy the desire for language.

These oscillations, or this narcissistic crisis, are conveyed through the transference. Somehow our doubts become burdened with certainty and fate. We worry about our qualifications, wondering, for instance, whether we have the right to teach, but then are certain that others have this right. We become anxious over whether we are able to withstand what we imagine the students want and become convinced that students are becoming more needy and less prepared. We wonder if the profession has already lost what some have called "the war of education," but may be puzzled at how besieged and overwhelmed we feel. These anxieties, mirrored through the projective identification of education, combine aggression with terrific idealizations. They are the conditions for doubt to transform itself into certainty and for the narcissistic crisis to confuse what Kristeva (1982) sees as "spatial ambivalence (inside/outside uncertainty) and an ambiguity of perception (pleasure/pain)" (62). What follows are feelings of loss and then a turning of the defense back upon the self: some of us will believe with a terrible conviction that there are no means we possess to overcome barriers to learning and the barriers are experienced as punishment for all that we lack. Many of these anxieties crowd out the desire to teach and more often than not our education may render us more helpless by its disavowal of its own feelings about helplessness, hate, and fear. We seem to forget the matter of subjectivity, or reduce it to the confines of technique, burdening newly arrived teachers with shiny rubrics, evidence-based teaching tips, and an avalanche of advice that foreclose the emotional storms and aesthetic conflicts that are constitutive features of working within uncertainty. This is another dimension of Winnicott's (1992) hate in the countertransference, when the educational institution, which is always made by people, treats its subjects as an empty vessel.

THE SUBJECT SUPPOSED TO KNOW

Lacan's (1998b) provocative formulation of "the subject supposed to know" is a story of what happens to us when we demand knowledge from the other because we believe the other already knows. But its address always misses its destination. As soon as there is a subject supposed to know, there is the transference, "bound up with desire as the nodal phenomenon of the human being" (231). The quest is impossible, for how can we actually possess the other's love and knowledge? It is an adventure in alienation since the "I think" cannot accompany this representation. Indeed, what is encountered is the nagging thought that absolute knowledge, a narcissistic knowledge without limit or vulnerability, is not only out of reach but belongs to someone else. In Lacan's view, one of the most difficult tasks of analysis and of thinking, whether it takes the form of theory or clinical practice, is the destruction, through interpretation, of "the subject presumed to know" (267). What is destroyed is identification. The terrible paradox is that the subject presumed to know, there in times of uncertainty, and when love is demanded, is also the condition for both thinking and obscurantism.

The subject supposed to know is a pernicious figure in the history of educational institutions and, as such, is a founding problem of what instructs pedagogy (Derrida 2002). There really is no word that orients thinking to the possibility of what it is that structures, precedes, and renders intelligible pedagogical action. There is no word that contains something like how the givenness of a pedagogical act is given. And our theories of pedagogy rarely venture into the question of why we have theory at all. Yet we imagine pedagogy as the accomplishment of the subject presumed to know. It is here that we exchange thinking for obscurantism and this is a feature of any field of knowledge. Adorno's (1991) review, "The Artist as Deputy," may be read as a commentary on the work of the impossible. I understood his essay as proposing philosophy as a fourth impossible profession. The essay discusses the poet Paul Valéry's study of the impressionist painter Degas to comment on the problem of thinking the impossible.

Adorno conjures an imagined reader who objects to his qualifications in taking on this topic. Readers, he writes, may take "offense when a philosopher talks about a book by an esoteric poet about a painter obsessed with craft" (101). The nature of the offense is more than who has the right to transgress so many academic boundaries, although at first glance this problem of qualification may concern some readers. However, it is the topic itself that will cause consternation since what Adorno is after is the destruction of reality as given and our feelings that we must adapt and comply to it. Adorno is most concerned with a transgression or alienation internal to the act of representing the thinking subject. Adapting to reality, he supposes, is like giving up on having to think. In Adorno's view, there can be no loyalty to an original object since thought itself is never adequate to the object, and since there is something tragic and comic about conceptualization as such. We cannot accompany our representations because of negation, bungled actions, and, a constitutive limit: the mind does not have the capacity to comment upon what its thinking does to thoughts. And thought can be neither reconciled by better language nor clarified with better knowledge. Thinking then is thinking antimony since it expresses its own limitations and cannot know its excess. The very act of thinking invokes the limit of thought.

Yet to meet Adorno's list of characters in his essay on Valéry—the philosopher, the esoteric poet, and the obsessed painter—may mean that we readers, too, must wonder if there is also made here transference with being "obsessed with craft" (101). After all, this obsession, however sublimated, signals a conflict with the nature of our own incompleteness. Adorno uses the esoteric poet and an impressionist artist, both of whom may be accused of wrecking reality, as a critique of the philosopher's thinking that can mistake its assertions for the object it seeks to know. Herein lies the problem. Adorno needs his imagined objector to pressure the essay from within to push his critique beyond the limit of accepted ideas of mastery, expertise, and even the ideal, so common to both the fields of art and philosophy, of the natural genius. These are the qualifications of the subject presumed to know. The cost of writing without qualification can be catastrophic. While commenting on Valéry's ideas on Degas, Adorno's simplest sentence is also advice: "It is better to be ruined attempting the impossible" (107). Here is where he summarized his own obsession as a revolt against the affirmations that congratulate the expert.

Adorno insists that great art and great philosophy demand from both spectator and creator a labor of thought that can think against itself. He may be asking us to write our own literature or perhaps to see in our labor an uncanny relation of nonidentity. Through this contradiction, the spectator must be willing to enter that which does not exist but presents as real. For the spectator, thinking itself becomes an act of creation and this act transforms the thinker, rather than the art encountered. As for the creator of the art, she or he must attempt the impossible by making something from nothing even as, in the words of Valéry:

> Each step forward makes it more beautiful and more remote. The idea of completely mastering the technique of an art, of achieving the freedom to employ its means as confidently and as easily as we do our limbs and our senses in their ordinary functions, is one which inspires a few men to infinite determination, struggle, practice, and agony. (Valéry cited in Adorno, 103)

The desire for art and the impossible mastery of its technique leads to the agony of trying to represent something that does not exist, yet still exerts a claim. Perhaps this identification with what has never existed is also reparation of sorts. Adorno suggests a new impossibility: that art and writing about it "acts as the representative of what we might one day be" (107). This transference then concerns the transfer of affects into creative acts. Artists and writers seem to accept the emotional situation that there are no promises for what tomorrow brings and they are still willing to risk inspiration and confidence. To become what we have never been is to wager our craft along with the obsessions that express, without qualification, a gigantic measure of our ignorance. Vulnerable to error and accidents and subject to radical indeterminacy, we wager our ignorance against "the subject supposed to know."

"MAKING THE BEST OF A BAD JOB"

Bion's (2000) last paper has the difficult title "Making the Best of a Bad Job." Its brevity presents to the impossible professions a new sense of both ignorance

THE IMPOSSIBLE PROFESSIONS

and impossibility. Bion does not mention education, although its beginning
tells us a great deal about the impossible professions' opening dilemma as well
as Klein's carnival of affect found in school:

> When two personalities meet, an emotional storm is created. If they make
> sufficient contact to be aware of each other, or even sufficient to be *un*aware
> of each other, an emotional state is produced by the conjunction of these
> two individuals, and the resulting disturbance is hardly to be regarded as
> necessarily an improvement on the state of affairs had they never met at all.
> But since they *have* met, and since this emotional storm has occurred, the
> two parties to this storm may decide to 'make the best of a bad job.' (321)

With or without awareness, whenever people meet, they create with each
other an emotional state. We might ask, "Who can live there?" This transference may well be our first emotional storm and the means for conveying
it. For the impossible professions, everything is at stake in what happens
here and, in this sense, the bad job Bion points to has more to do with our
capacity to meet at all, to make contact with one another, than it does with
the work itself.

So while Bion begins with these hurt feelings, adding more to Freud's
view of our affected professions, he advises that the analyst's work will consist
in trying to further this emotional contact which he believes is the basis for
creating a "good account" (322). How hurt feelings can be noticed and used
is always the question. Part of a good account, I believe, depends on thinking of affect as revelatory and as indicating a collapse of our pedagogical or
therapeutic theme. Symbolizing emotional storms is the inevitable work of the
impossible professions, and, in my view, this is the responsibility that their
education must learn to represent. And giving a good account as to what is
happening when we meet may encourage us to ask our own questions, beginning with "how am I to learn?"

Our educational challenges are great, contributing interminable feelings to the impossible professions and thus their need for self-analysis. Perhaps
what is most impossible is the question: what do we understand about our
own ignorance? The wager for education in the professions is whether we
can stand the ideas and feelings made when ignorance takes its own novel
time, not as passion for itself, not as narcissistic defense, and not as disclaiming
affect and our impressive subjectivity. Rather, what if our education helped
us understand ignorance as a condition of *not actually knowing*. The paradox
is that not knowing can be represented through the wandering mind and the
unconscious, which opens a potential space that our instituted education, in

its own passion for ignorance, more often than not, fears and even hates. This is education's secret narcissism. When emotional contact is feared and reality is treated as compliance, education's depressive anxiety reverts to its paranoid/ schizoid position, a terrible anxiety where too much is known, fixed, and certain. Admitting that we actually do not know what may occur as we go about learning our work may well add a third dimension to McDougall's ethic of psychic survival. Recall that this ethic suggests our obligation is to attempt to encourage psychic creativity and an awareness of how it may be destroyed. I believe we can add to this the paradox of representing *not knowing* as a means to open psychic survival to its own otherness and to consider this ignorance as where we learn to tolerate, without qualification, affect's revelatory potential.

Bion proposes a difficult ignorance made when we meet one another. He believes we learn and meet the other only with "half our wits about us" (329). There are at least three sides to his Oepidal claim. First, we may wonder which half of our wits is being conveyed through our work. Second, Bion may have been referencing the radical uncertainty created when two people meet that he calls "emotional storms" (321). On this view, two halves do not make a whole. And third, he may be greeting the unconscious, that other place of half our wits, the one hardly known yet nonetheless insists on laughing. In my view, one of the large problems we face when trying to make the best of a bad job is whether we can stand the very thought of this indeterminacy as our education, as the element without qualification, and as the condition that grants to our imagination the grace needed for its therapeutics. After all, even with our Achilles' heel, we can still walk.

NOTES

NOTES TO CHAPTER ONE

1. Bion (1997) writes: "If a thought without a thinker comes along, it may be what is a 'stray thought', or it could be a thought with the owner's name and address on it, or it could be a 'wild thought.' The problem, should such a thought come along, is what to do with it" (27). Later in this short untitled essay, Bion recalls his own dreamy childhood states of "idling way my time, thinking in this way—a way I could describe as being almost thoughtless. If, as a child, I had been caught at it, somebody would have said, 'Why on earth don't you find something to do?'" (32). Indeed, why on earth do we dream?

NOTES TO CHAPTER FIVE

1. A great deal of discussion occurs on the idea of emotional intelligence and the teacher's need to develop with students the mastery of positive thoughts and motivation. For an example of this approach, see, for instance, Goleman (2000). Pitt and Brushwood-Rose (2007) have formulated a stringent critique of its use in educational settings, suggesting that the application of the measures of emotional intelligence "may appeal to educators because it responds to important worries without straining at or placing under scrutiny education's dream of knowing what the problem is and how to solve it" (2). In other words, emotional intelligence cannot arrive at the problem of its signification. I'll set this discourse aside to propose a psychoanalytic orientation to the symbolization of the teacher's affect.

2. Kant (1965) argued that human knowledge has two irreducible sources: objects given to perception and thoughts about them. "Without sensibility no object would be given to us, without understanding no object would be thought. Thoughts without content are empty, intuition without concepts are blind" (93). Bion (1993b) would use Kant's formulation for his idea of "thoughts without a thinker" (165) and "empty thoughts" (111).

3. The word "object" is one of the most problematic terms in psychoanalysis, partly because in everyday use the object is associated with objectification and thingness and is a way to oppose the subject and partly because there is not much agreement

on the valence of the term. It refers to what is outside the self, objects of attraction and disgust taken into the self, forming phantasies of the world and of others. The object can be a "part object" referring to bodily zones and its libidinal aims. Although it is partial, for Klein the object refers to the ways aspects of others are identified with and endowed by phantasies of a person's dynamics such as aggression, hate love, and goodness. In this sense, objects constitute object relations. They are unstated yet enacted theories of being with others, and are given their afterlife phantasy. To distinguish this mental constellation, I follow Klein's spelling: *ph*antasy.

4. Aulagnier (2001) proposes as a developmental achievement of children the idea of secret thinking when they realize a statement of the mother can be doubted and questioned without her knowing that.

> For this choice to be made, a minimum of autonomy in thinking must be accorded the I from the outset; the first result of this autonomy will be the ability to think secretly. . . . It is a pleasure that is reinforced by the unexpected discovery that, despite the little real power possessed at this stage in terms of bodily autonomy, despite one's state of dependence for the satisfaction of one's needs, despite the vital demand for love to which one is subjected, *in the register of thinking the Mother may be just as much at your mercy as you are at hers.* (152–153)

Secret thinking, on this view, is never given up, but the pleasure attained is contradictory since while secret thinking allows the pleasure at having one's own mind, a part of the pleasure is tied to the child's aggression made in relation to the other who cannot acknowledge and may even punish the child for having her or his own mind. What is secret about these thoughts are feelings of hostility and pleasure.

5. I have borrowed the word "tailpiece" from Winnicott (2001), who ends his book with a short paradox concerning the theoretical beginnings of the infant, itself a strange use of theoretical since it references what is there but is yet to be made. This tension is what Winnicott calls "the conception-perception gap" (151).

6. The early history of countertransference as an individual failing of the analyst to contain her anxieties, has affected, for some, the ways clinical work is written about. Bolognini (2001) for example, suggests that not only must the analyst's "good" veneer be disillusioned, but also one of the greatest challenges is trying to understand the truth of one's feelings as it relates to the one who feels: "What an analyst is called on to do . . . if conscientiously invested in the countertransference work of self-analysis, is to tell himself the truth, beyond any idealization and in the interests of his own patients. This is both our right and our obligation" (129).

NOTES TO CHAPTER SIX

1. Hilda Doolittle (1886–1961), born in the United States, was a modernist poet, translator, and essayist who lived most of her life in the UK. She was involved

with the modernist literary movement, itself an attempt to open language—through cinema, dance, poetry, literature, visual arts, theater, and music—to its symbolic conflicts. In the time frame of my essay, H.D. was immersed in psychoanalytic circles in London, Berlin, and Vienna. Her friendship with Havelock Ellis and support from her longtime companion, Bryher, gave her entrance into Freud's psychoanalytic practice. For a robust, scholarly discussion of her life and her circle of friends in relation to the letters she wrote, see Friedman 2002. For what is perhaps the first discussion of H.D.'s testimony to Freud from the vantage of what Rose (1986) has called the "vexed relation between actuality, memory, fantasy which is the domain of the Freudian unconscious" (14), and then the impasse made during the analysis, see Rose 1986. My reading of Freud's request that H.D. never defend him departs from Rose's discussion since I am interested in what it might mean to defend psychoanalysis without becoming defensive, or proposing a defense of psychoanalysis as a defense of the imagination and its freedom.

2. The phrasing "transference people" was the result of my libidinal misreading of Meltzer and William's (1988) chapter on love at first sight. It describes our capacity for passionate emotional attachment to strangers and the accompanying wish for beautiful, magical intimacy. It is the first rush of the mind in love with a stranger that caused me to fall, headlong, into my misreading. The sentence is: "Our minds are full of characters in search—not of an author, for we ourselves are the author—but of players to fit the part. Thus does transference people the intimate area of our lives" (38). So, you see, it is not "transference people" but the idea that the purpose of the transference is not just to project our style of loving into the other, but also to take others, including their style of loving, into our minds.

3. Freud's work, along with others, was publicly burned in Berlin on May 10, 1933. Just three years earlier, in 1930, Freud traveled to Berlin, a lively center for both psychoanalysis and the arts. His trip is documented in the correspondence with Jones, but one can also see today a picture of Freud boarding a plane in Berlin in 1930 found on the Berlin homepage of the Freud Lacan Society. (See Paskauskas 1995 for the correspondence and www.freud-lacan-berlin.de for the picture.) Whereas in 1933 Freud's books were burned, the Jewish Museum of Berlin held an exhibition (April 7–September 22, 2006) celebrating Sigmund Freud's 150th birthday. (See www. juedisches-museum-berlin.de). Edmundson's (2007) study of Freud's last years details Freud's life in Vienna during the Nazi takeover and his reception in London during his last year of life. The study is noteworthy in so many ways; perhaps the main one concerns Freud's relentless interest in the problem of thinking as a means to respond to instinct and fundamentalism in politics and in religion.

4. *Entartete Musik* or degenerate, unnatural music consists of works by composers suppressed or displaced during 1930–1940 in the Third Reich. Decca Record Company Limited, London, has released a series of recordings under this name, which spans opera, operetta, symphonic and chamber music, as well as cabaret and music influenced by African American jazz and South American dance. Most, but not all, of

the music was made by Jewish composers. In 1938, the Nazis staged an exhibition of this forbidden music in Dusseldorf. They also held an exhibition in Munich of *Entartete Kunst* (Degenerate Art) (see Dümling, 1993).

5. Walter did conduct in Vienna during 1933 and H.D. may have seen him in performance as she often went to both the symphony and the opera during her stay there. Walter was considered one of the foremost interpreters of German music. He was based in Vienna from 1933 to 1936, where his programming at the Vienna Philharmonic during those years ranged from Kurt Weil's symphonies to Beethoven and Mahler. In 1935, Walter published a pamphlet, "On the Moral Forces of Music" in which he argued that music's toleration of dissonance has the potential to bring out the best in humanity (see Ryding and Pechefsky 2001, 240–248). In 1936, Nazis disturbed his performance with the Viennese Philharmonic in Vienna and Walter received a death threat for a concert there with Marian Anderson. He left with his family that year, eventually to settle in the United States.

6. I am grateful to Sharon Sliwinski for pointing out this published interview and to Alice Pitt for her German translations. As we walked in the Jewish Museum of Berlin in October 2006, Pitt pointed out the Arendt televised interview and translated from German to English what Arendt said (see Arendt 2005).

7. Foucault's (2001) lecture on *Ion* presents this play from the vantage of the Greek *Parrhesias* or the capacity to speak the truth freely or to speak freely to care for the self. *Ion* was a breakthrough play in that it is not the Greek gods who tell mortals the truth but rather that there is now a human struggle for the truth. Foucault puts it this way: "human beings must manage, by themselves to discover and tell the truth" (44). While not citing H.D.'s translation at all, like H.D., Foucault uses this play as a portal to our contemporary problems with telling the truth, free speech, and living an artistic life, which for Foucault concerned care of the self. He leaves us with the question of education: "What is the importance of telling the truth, knowing who is able to tell the truth, and knowing why we should tell the truth?" (170).

REFERENCES

Adorno, Theodor W. 1991. The artist as deputy. In *Notes to literature*. Vol. 1. Trans. Sherry Weber Nicholsen and ed. Rolf Tiedemann. 98–108. New York: Columbia University Press.

———. 1992. *Mahler: A musical physiognomy*. Trans. Edmund Jephcott. Chicago: University of Chicago Press.

———. 1998. Education after Auschwitz. In *Critical models: interventions and catchwords*. Trans. Henry W. Pickford. 191–204. New York: Columbia University Press.

———. 2001. *Kant's critique of pure reason*. Trans. Rodney Livingstone and ed. Rolf Tiedemann. Stanford: Stanford University Press.

———. 2006. *History and freedom: lectures 1964–1965*. Trans. Rodney Livingstone and ed. Rolf Tiedemann. Malden, MA: Polity Press.

———. 2007. *Dream notes*. Trans. Rodney Livingstone and ed. Christoph Gödde and Henri Lonitz. Malden, MA: Polity Press.

Agamben, Giorgio. 2007. *Infancy and history: on the destruction of experience*. Trans. Liz Heron. London: Verso.

Aichhorn, August. 1983. *Wayward youth*. New York: Northwestern University Press.

Arendt, Hannah. 1958. *The human condition*. Chicago: University of Chicago Press.

———. 1993a. *Between past and future: eight exercises in political thought*. New York: Penguin Books.

———. 1993b. The crisis of education. In *Between past and future: eight exercises in political thought*. 173–196. New York: Penguin Books.

———. 2005. What remains? The language remains: A conversation with Gunter Gaus. In *Essays in understanding, 1930–1954: formation, exile, and totalitarianism*. Ed. Jerome Kohn. 1–23. New York: Schocken Books.

Aulagnier, Piera. 2001. *The violence of interpretation: from pictogram to statement*. Trans. Alan Sheridan. London: Brunner-Routledge.

Badiou, Alain. 2005. *Handbook of inaesthetics*. Trans. Alberto Toscano. Stanford: Stanford University Press.

Bass, Alan. 1998. Sigmund Freud: the question of a weltanschauung and of defence. In *Psychoanalytic versions of the human condition: philosophies of life and their impact on practice*. Ed. Paul Marcus and Alan Rosenberg. 412–446. New York: New York University Press.

————. 2000. *Difference and disavowal: The trauma of Eros*. Stanford: Stanford University Press.

Bick, Ester. 1987. Teacher, counsellor, therapist: toward a definition of the roles. 1972. In *The collected papers of Martha Harris and Ester Bick*. Ed. Meg Harris Williams. 311–321. Pershire: Rolland Harris Educational Trust.

————. 1996. Child analysis today. 1962. In *Melanie Klein today: developments in theory and practice*. Vol. 2, *Mainly Practice*. Ed. Elizabeth Bott Spillius. 168–176. London: Routledge.

Bion, Wilfred. 1993a. A theory of thinking. In *Second thoughts: selected papers on psychoanalysis*. 110–119. London: Karnac Books.

————. 1993b. *Second thoughts: selected papers on psychoanalysis*. London: Karnac Books.

————. 1994a. *Experiences in groups, and other papers*. London: Routledge.

————. 1994b. *Learning from experience*. Northvale, NJ: Jason Aronson.

————. 1997. *Taming wild thoughts*. Ed. Francesca Bion. London: Karnac Books.

————. 2000. Making the best of a bad job. 1979. In *Clinical seminars and other works*. 321-331. London: Karnac Books.

Bird, Brian. 1990. Notes on transference. In *Essential papers on transference*. Ed. Aaron H. Esman. 331–361. New York: New York University Press.

Bolognini, Stefano. 2001. The'kind-hearted' versus the good analyst: empathy and hatred in the countertransference. In *Squiggles and spaces*. Vol 2, *Revisiting the work of D. W. Winnicott*. Trans. Don Var Green and Anthony Molino, ed. Mario Bertolini, Andreas Giannakoulas, and Max Hernandez. 120–129. London: Whurr.

Britzman, Deborah P. 1998. *Lost subjects, contested objects: toward a psychoanalytic inquiry of learning*. Albany: State University of New York Press.

————. 2003a. *After-education: Anna Freud, Melanie Klein and psychoanalytic histories of learning*. Albany: State University of New York Press.

————. 2003b. *Practice makes practice: A critical study of learning to teach*. Rev. ed. Albany: State University of New York Press.

————. 2006. *Novel education: psychoanalytic studies of learning and not learning*. New York: Peter Lang.

Butler, Judith. 1997. *The psychic life of power: theories of subjection*. Stanford: Stanford University Press.

————. 2005. *Giving an account of oneself*. New York: Fordham University Press.

Copjec, Joan. 1994. Introduction. In *Supposing the subject*. Ed. J. Copjec. vii–xiii. London: Verso.

Derrida, Jacques. 1994. *Specters of Marx: the state of the debt, the work of mourning, and the new international*. Trans. Peggy Kamuf. New York: Routledge.

————. 1998. *Resistances of psychoanalysis*. Trans. Peggy Kamuf, Pascale-Anne Brault and Michael Nass. Stanford: Stanford University Press.

————. 2002. *Who's afraid of philosophy? Right to philosophy*. Trans. Jan Plug. Stanford: Stanford University Press.

Doidge, Norman. 2007. *The brain that changes itself: stories of personal triumph from the frontiers of brain science.* New York: Viking.

Dümling, Albrecht. 1993. The significance of "Entartete Musik" for the past and the present. In Korngold's *Das Wunder der Heliane.* Trans. Phillip Weller. Decca recording. B Schott's Sohne, Mainz, Germany.

Edmundson, Mark. 2007. *The death of Sigmund Freud: the legacy of his last days.* New York: Bloomsbury USA.

Feder, Stuart. 2004. *Gustav Mahler: A life in crisis.* New Haven: Yale University Press.

Felman, Shoshana. 1987. *Jacques Lacan and the adventure of insight: psychoanalysis in contemporary culture.* Cambridge: Harvard University Press.

———. 2003. *Writing and madness: literature/philosophy/psychoanalysis.* Trans. Martha Noel Evans. Stanford: Stanford University Press.

Fink, Bruce. 2002. Knowledge and jouissance. In *Reading Seminar XX: Lacan's major work on love, knowledge, and feminine sexuality.* Ed. Suzanne Bernard and Bruce Fink. 21–46. New York: State University of New York Press.

Fodor, Jerry. 2007. Headaches have themselves: A review of "Consciousness and its Place in Nature," by Galen Strawson. In *London Review of Books.* 29(10): May 24, 9–10.

Forman, Maurice Buxton, ed. 1960. *The letters of John Keats.* 4th ed. London: Oxford Univ. Press.

Foucault, Michel. 2001. *Fearless speech.* Ed. Joseph Pearson. Los Angeles: Semiotext(e).

———. 2005. *The hermeneutics of the subject: lectures at the Collège de France, 1981–1982.* Trans. Graham Burchell and ed. Frederic Gros. New York: Palgrave-Macmillan.

———. 2006. *History of madness.* Trans. Jonathan Murphy and Jean Khalfa and ed. Jean Khalfa. New York: Routledge.

Freud, Anna. 1974. Four lectures on psychoanalysis for teachers and parents. 1930. In *The Writings of Anna Freud.* Vol. 1, *Introduction to psychoanalysis and lectures for child analysts and teachers.* 1922–1935. 73–133. New York: International Universities Press.

———. 1995. The ego and the mechanisms of defence. 1936. In *The writings of Anna Freud.* Vol. 2, *The ego and the mechanisms of defense,* rev. ed. Trans. and revised Cecil Baines. Madison: International Universities Press.

———. 1969. Doctoral Award Address. 1967[1964]. In *The writings of Anna Freud.* Vol. 5, *Research at the Hampstead Child-Therapy Clinic and Other Papers, 1956–1965.* 507–516. New York: International Universities Press.

Freud, Sigmund. 1968. *The standard edition of the complete psychological works of Sigmund Freud.* Trans. and ed. James Strachey, in collaboration with Anna Freud, assisted by Alix Strachey and Alan Tyson. 24 vols. London: Hogarth Press and Institute for Psychoanalysis.

———. *The interpretation of dreams (Second Part).* 1900. Vol. 5. 339–632.

———. *The psychopathology of everyday life.* 1901. Vol. 6. 1–310.

———. *Creative writers and day-dreaming.* 1908. Vol. 9. 141–153.

———. *The future prospects of psycho-analytic therapy.* 1910. Vol. 11. 139–151.

———. *The dynamics of transference.* 1912. Vol. 12. 97–108.

———. *Remembering, repeating and working through (Further recommendations on the technique of psycho-analysis. II).* 1914a. Vol. 12. 145–156.

———. *Formulations on the two principles of mental functioning.* 1911. Vol. 12. 215–226.

———. *Some reflections of schoolboy psychology.* 1914b. Vol. 13. 241–244.

———. *On transience.* 1916. Vol. 14. 303–308.

———. *On the teaching of psycho-analysis in universities.* 1919. Vol. 17. 171–173.

———. *The ego and the id.* 1923. Vol. 19. 3–66.

———. *The resistance to psycho-analysis.* 1925a. Vol. 19. 212–222.

———. *Negation.* 1925b. Vol. 19. 235–239.

———. *Preface to Aichhorn's "Wayward Youth."* 1925c. Vol. 19. 273–275.

———. *Civilization and its discontents.* 1930 [1929]. Vol. 21. 64–145.

———. *New introductory lectures on psycho-analysis.* 1933 [1932]. Vol. 22. 5–182.

———. *Analysis terminable and interminable.* 1937. Vol. 23. 209–254.

Freud, Sigmund, and C. G. Jung. 1974. *The Freud/Jung letters: the correspondence between Sigmund Freud and C. G. Jung.* Trans. Ralph Manheim and R. F. C. Hull and ed. W. McGuire. Princeton: Princeton University Press.

Frie, Roger, ed. 2003. *Understanding experience: psychotherapy and postmodernism.* New York: Routledge.

Friedman, Susan Stanford, ed. 2002. *Analyzing Freud: letters of H.D., Bryher, and their circle.* New York: New Directions Books.

Goleman, Daniel. 2000. *Working with emotional intelligence.* New York: Bantan.

Green, André. 1999. *The fabric of affect in the psychoanalytic discourse.* Trans. Alan Sheridan. London: Routledge.

———. 2000. Experience and thinking in analytic practice. In *André Green at the Squiggle Foundation.* Ed. Jan Abram. 1–15. London: Karnac Books.

Greene, Maxine. 1973. *Teacher as stranger: educational philosophy for the modern age.* Belmont, Calif: Wadsworth.

H. D. 1974. *Tribute to Freud: writing on the wall and advent.* New York: New Directions.

———. 2003. Ion. In *Hippolytus temporizes and Ion: adaptations of two plays by Euripides.* 145–261. New York: New Directions.

Hullot-Kentor, Robert. 2006. *Things beyond resemblance: collected essays on Theodor W. Adorno.* New York: Columbia University Press.

Infante, Jose A. 1995. Some reflections on phantasy and creativity. In *On Freud's "Creative writers and day-dreaming."* Ed. Ethel Spector, Peter Fonagy, and Servulo Augusto Figueira. 53–64. New Haven: Yale University.

Ishiguro, Kazuo. 2005. *Never let me go.* Toronto: Knopf.

Jacobus, Mary. 1999. *Psychoanalysis and the scene of reading.* Oxford: Oxford University Press.

———. 2005. *The poetics of psychoanalysis: in the wake of Klein.* Oxford: Oxford University Press.

James, William. 1950. *The principles of psychology*. 1890. Vol. 1 and 2. New York: Dover.

———. 1983. *Talks to teachers on psychology and to students on some of life's ideals*. 1899. Cambridge: Harvard University Press.

Jersild, Arthur Thomas. 1955. *When teachers face themselves*. New York: Teachers College Press.

Joseph, Betty. 1997. On understanding and not understanding: some technical issues. 1983. In *Psychic equilibrium and psychic change selected papers of Betty Joseph*. Ed. Michael Feldman, and Elizabeth Bott Spillius. London: Routledge Press.

Kant, Immanuel. 1965. *The critique of pure reason*. Trans. Norman Kemp Smith. Unabridged ed. New York: St. Martin's Press.

Klein, Melanie. 1975. The importance of symbol-formation in the development of the ego. 1930. In *Love, guilt, and reparation & other works, 1921–1945*. Vol. 1. 219–232. New York: Delacorte/Seymour Lawrence.

———. 1975. A contribution to the theory of intellectual inhibition. 1931. In *Love, guilt, and reparation & other works, 1921–1945*. 236–248. New York: Delacorte/Seymour Lawrence.

———. 1975. The significance of early anxiety-situations in the development of the ego. 1932. In *The psychoanalysis of children*. Vol. 2. Trans. Alix Strachey. 176–195. London: Hogarth Press.

———. 1975. A contribution to the psychogenesis of manic-depressive states. 1935. In *Love, guilt, and reparation & other works, 1921–1945*. Vol. 1. 262–289. New York: Delacorte/Seymour Lawrence.

———. 1964. Love, guilt and reparation. 1937. In *Love, hate and reparation*. By Melanie Klein and Joan Rivere. 57–119. New York: Norton.

———. 1975. Mourning and its relation to manic-depressive states. 1940. In *Love, guilt, and reparation & other works, 1921–1945*. Vol. 1. 344–369. New York: Delacorte/Seymour Lawrence.

———. 1975. Notes on some schizoid mechanisms. 1946. In *Envy and gratitude and other works, 1946–1963*. Vol. 3. 1–24. New York: Delcorte/Seymour Lawrence.

———. 1975. Some theoretical conclusions regarding the emotional life of the infant. 1952. In *Envy and gratitude and other works, 1946–1963*. Vol. 3. 61–93. New York: Delcorte/Seymour Lawrence.

———. 1975. Envy and gratitude. 1957. In *Envy and gratitude, and other works, 1946–1963*. Vol. 3. 176–235. London: Delacorte/Seymour Lawrence.

Kofman, Sarah. 2007a. The impossible profession. In *Selected writings of Sarah Kofman*. Trans. Patience Moll and ed. Thomas Albecht, Georgia Albert, and Elizabeth Rottenberg. 56–70. Stanford: Stanford University Press.

———. 2007b. "My life" and psychoanalysis. In *Selected writings of Sarah Kofman*. Trans. Patience Moll and ed. Thomas Albecht, Georgia Albert, and Elizabeth Rottenberg. 250–251. Stanford: Stanford University Press.

Kohon, Gregorio. 1986a. Notes on the history of the psychoanalytic movement in Great Britain. In *The British School of psychoanalysis: the Independent tradition*. 24–50. Ed. Gregorio Kohon. London: Free Association Books.

———. 1986b. Countertransference: An Independent view. In *The British School of psychoanalysis: the Independent tradition*. 51–73. Ed. Gregorio Kohon. London: Free Association Books.

———. 2005. Love in a time of madness. In *Love and its vicissitudes*. Ed. André Green and Gregorio Kohon. 43–100. London: Routledge.

———. 2007. Borderline traces and the question of diagnosis. In *Resonance of suffering: countertransference in non-neurotic structures*. Ed. André Green. 203–215. London: International Psychoanalytic Association.

Kristeva, Julia. 1982. *Powers of horror: An essay on abjection*. Trans. Leon S. Roudiez. New York: Columbia University Press.

———. 1989. *Black sun: depression and melancholia*. Trans. Leon S. Roudiez. New York: Columbia University Press.

———. 1991. *Strangers to ourselves*. Trans. Leon S. Roudiz. New York: Columbia University Press.

———. 1998. Psychoanalysis and freedom. Trans. Charles Levin. *Canadian Journal of Psychoanalysis* 7(1):1–21.

———. 2001. *Melanie Klein*. Trans. Ross Guberman. New York: Columbia University Press.

———. 2007. Adolescence, a syndrome of ideality. Trans. Michael Marder and Patricia I. Vieira. *Psychoanalytic Review*, 94(5):715–725.

Lacan, Jacques. 1998a. *Encore. On feminine sexuality: the limits of love and knowledge*. 1972–1973. Bk. 20. *The seminar of Jacques Lacan*. Trans. Bruce Fink and ed. Jacques-Alain Miller. New York: Norton.

———. 1998b. *The four fundamental concepts of psycho-analysis*. Bk. 11. *The seminar of Jacques Lacan*. Trans. Alan Sheridan and ed. Jacques-Alain Miller. New York: Norton.

———. 2006a. The direction of the treatment and the principles of power. In *Ecrits: the first complete edition in English*. Trans. Bruce Fink in collaboration with Heloise Fink and Russell Grigg. 489–542. New York: Norton.

———. 2006b. The situation of psychoanalysis and the training of psychoanalysis in 1956. In *Ecrits*. Trans. Bruce Fink in collaboration with Heloise Fink and Russell Grigg. 384–407. New York: Norton.

Laplanche, Jean. 1999. The drive and its source-object: its fate in the transference. In *Essays on otherness*. Ed. John Fletcher. 117–132. London: Routledge.

Lear, Jonathan. 2003. *Therapeutic action: An earnest plea for irony*. New York: Other Press.

———. 2006. *Radical hope: ethics in the face of cultural devastation*. Cambridge: Harvard University Press.

Loewald, Hans. 2000a. Some considerations on repetition and repetition compulsion. In *The essential Loewald: collected papers and monographs*. 87–101. Hagerstown, MD: University Pub. Group.

———. 2000b. On the therapeutic action of psychoanalysis. 1960. *The essential Loewald: collected papers and monographs*. 221–256. Hagerstown, MD: University Pub. Group.

Lyotard, Jean François. 1987. *The postmodern condition: A report on knowledge.* Trans. Geoff Bennington and Brian Massumi. Manchester: Manchester University Press.

Mann, Thomas. 2005. *The magic mountain.* 1924. Trans. John E. Woods. New York: Knopf.

McDougall, Joyce. 1995. *The many faces of Eros: A psychoanalytic exploration of human sexuality.* New York: Norton.

Meltzer, Donald. 1992. *The claustrum: An investigation of claustrophobic phenomena.* London: Roland Harris Education Trust.

Meltzer, Donald, and Meg Harris Williams. 1988. *The apprehension of beauty: the role of aesthetic conflict in development, violence and art.* Worcester: Clunie Press.

———. 2004. Aesthetic conflict: its place in the developmental process. In *Psychoanalysis and art: Kleinian perspectives.* Ed. Sandra Gosso. 178–200. London: Karnac Books.

Molino, Anthony, ed. 1997. *Freely associated encounters in psychoanalysis.* London: Free Association Books.

Newcombe, Rachel. 2007. Beyond redemption. *Psychoanalytic Review*, 94(3):447–461.

Paskauskas, R. Andrew, ed. 1995. *The complete correspondence of Sigmund Freud and Ernest Jones, 1908–1939.* Cambridge: Harvard University Press.

Phillips, Adam. 2006. Introduction. In *Sigmund Freud: the Penguin Freud reader.* vii–xv. New York: Penguin.

Pitt, Alice J., and Chloe Brushwood-Rose. 2007. The significance of emotions in teaching and learning: on making emotional significance. *International Journal of Leadership in Education,* 10:1–11.

Polk, Richard. 2006. *The emergency of being: on Heidegger's contributions to philosophy.* Ithaca: Cornell University Press.

Powers, Richard. 2006. *The echo maker.* New York: Farrar, Straus and Giroux.

Racker, Heinrich. 2002. *Transference and counter-transference.* London: Karnac Press.

Readings, Bill. 1996. *The university in ruins.* Cambridge: Harvard University Press.

Richardson, Robert D. 2006. *William James: in the maelstrom of American modernism.* Boston: Houghton Mifflin.

Ricœur, Paul. 2004. *Memory, history, forgetting.* Trans. Kathleen Blamey and David Pellauer. Chicago: University of Chicago Press.

———. 2005. *The course of recognition.* Trans. David Pellauer. Cambridge: Harvard University Press.

Riviere, Joan. 1964. Hate, greed and aggression. 1937. In *Love, hate and reparation.* By Melanie Klein and Joan Riviere. 3–56. New York: Norton.

Rose, Jacqueline. 1986. *Sexuality in the field of vision.* London: Verso.

———. 1993. *Why war? Psychoanalysis, politics, and the return to Melanie Klein.* Oxford: Blackwell.

Roth, Joseph. 2003. *What I saw: reports from Berlin, 1920–1933.* Trans. Michael Hofmann. German selection by Michael Bienert. New York: Norton.

Rottenberg, Elizabeth. 2005. *Inheriting the future: legacies of Kant, Freud, and Flaubert.* Stanford: Stanford University Press.

Ruti, Mari. 2006. *Reinventing the soul: posthumanist theory and psychic life.* New York: Other Press.

Ryding, Erik, and Rebecca Pechefsky. 2001. *Bruno Walter: A world elsewhere.* New Haven: Yale University Press.

Santer, Eric L. 2001. *On the psychotheology of everyday life: reflections on Freud and Rosenzweig.* Chicago: University of Chicago Press.

Sedgwick, Eve Kosofsky. 1997. Paranoid reading and reparative reading; or you're so paranoid, you probably think this introduction is about you. In *Novel gazing: queer readings in fiction.* Ed. Eve Kosofsky Sedwick. 1–37. Durham: Duke University Press.

Slavitt, David R. 2007. Translator's preface. In *The Theban plays of Sophocles.* Trans. David Slavitt. ix–xi. New Haven: Yale University Press.

Steiner, George. 1980. On difficulty. In *On difficulty, and other essays.* 18–47. Oxford: Oxford University Press.

Strachey, James. 1990. The nature of the therapeutic action of psycho-analysis. 1934. In *Essential papers on transference.* Ed. Aaron Esman. 49–79. New York: New York University Press.

Turkle, Sherry. Diary. In *London Review of Books.* 28:8 (April 20, 2006), 36–37.

Urribarri, Fernando. 2007. The analyst's psychic work: And the three concepts of countertransference. In *Resonance of suffering: countertransference in non-neurotic structures.* Ed. André Green. 165–186. London: International Psychoanalytic Association.

von Unwerth, Matthew. 2005. *Freud's requiem: mourning, memory, and the invisible history of a summer walk.* New York: Riverhead Books.

Walter, Bruno. 1961. *Of music and music-making.* Trans. Paul Hamburger. New York: Norton.

———. 1966. *Theme and variations, an autobiography.* Trans. James Galston. New York: Knopf.

Winnicott, D. W. 1986a. The theory of parent–infant relationship. 1960. In *The maturational processes and the facilitating environment: studies in the theory of emotional development.* 37–55. Madison, CT: International Universities Press.

———. 1986b. The aims of psycho-analytical treatment. 1962. In *The maturational processes and the facilitating environment studies in the theory of emotional development.* 166–170. Madison, CT: International Universities Press.

———. 1987. Dependence in child care. 1970. In *Babies and their mothers.* Ed. Clare Winnicott, Ray Shepherd, and Madeleine Davis. 83–88. Reading, MA: Addison-Wesley.

———. 1988. Counter-transference. 1960. In *Essential papers on countertransference.* Ed. Benjamin Wolstein. 262–269. New York: New York University Press.

———. 1992. Hate in the countertransference. 1947. In *Through paediatrics to psycho-analysis: collected papers.* 194–203. New York: Brunner/Mazel.

———. 1996. Yes, but how do we know it's true? 1950. In *Thinking about children*. Ed. Jennifer Johns, Ray Shepherd, and Helen Taylor Robinson. 13–21. Reading, MA: Addison-Wesley.

———. 2001. Tailpiece. In *Playing and reality*. 151. Philadelphia, PA: Brunner-Routledge.

Wolstein, Benjamin. 1988. Introduction. In *Essential papers on countertransference*. 1–15. New York: New York University Press.

INDEX